How to
CALL
WILDLIFE

AN OUTDOOR LIFE BOOK

How to
CALL
WILDLIFE

Byron W. Dalrymple

OUTDOOR LIFE • FUNK & WAGNALLS
New York

Library of Congress Catalog Card Number: 74-33568
Funk & Wagnalls Hardcover Edition: ISBN 0-308-10208-8
Paperback Edition: ISBN 0-308-10209-6

Fifth Printing, 1978

Designed by Jeff Fitschen

Manufactured in the United States of America

Contents

How to
CALL
WILDLIFE

What It's All About

WHEN MY TWO SONS were small they were reading a book one morning that contained a story about a fox. That afternoon as we were driving on our ranch, one of them asked me if I thought any foxes lived there. I told them I was sure they did. I had, in fact, seen tracks often in some of our trails.

"Would you like to see one?" I asked. "Maybe we might."

They were much excited. The afternoon was breezeless. I stopped the vehicle, motioned them to silence. We got out and moved with stealth some distance down the trail. Then I carefully and quietly led them into a juniper thicket from which we could watch the trail but remain well hidden from view of our intended quarry.

Even youngsters can learn to call wildlife. Here a gray fox responds to the sounds of a rabbit in distress.

I had in my pocket a fox call. It was the kind you blow on. The reed was so adjusted that the squalling sound presumably imitated the anguished cries of an injured rabbit. I blew the call several times, then paused. I was just raising it again to my lips when a handsome gray fox came larruping down the trail toward our hiding place. It stopped, looked craftily around. I put my palm to my lips and made a very low squeaking or kissing sound. The fox crept closer, closer, until it was within mere feet.

One of the boys, unable to contain amazement, nudged the other and said, "Look at that!" With a growl the fox almost turned inside out in its haste to leave. The storybook at home got little attention thereafter. They had a real-life tale far more appealing to tell.

In the entire world of the outdoors there is no endeavor more exciting, none with more dramatic results, than the art of calling wildlife. The origins of this quite ancient, multiple art were in hunting. Not sport hunting, but hunting for food, and skins for clothing and other uses. Hundreds of years ago man contrived ways to allay the fears of wild creatures, so that he might approach them closely, or by means of certain sounds or varied representations actually bring animals and birds to him.

Almost all present-day knowledge of attracting birds and animals thus is based on hunting. Modern sport hunters have borrowed from early peoples and from their own more immediate ancestors. Sport hunters have added much clever technology and many ingenious devices, and they have refined calling truly to a high art. However, although presently it is the hunter, as it always has been, who most utilizes these crafty ruses, calling holds vast opportunity and interest for the nonhunter also.

Bird watchers, for example, are just now beginning to realize that broad new dimensions in calling should and can be achieved for their advantage and enjoyment, and for scientific purposes. Photographers are already using calls to produce better, and closer, pictures of wildlife. This in itself is a thrilling hobby, but still is in its infancy. Many nonhunting camera buffs have still not caught on to its potential. Calling to observe wild creatures and watch their reactions is also a hobby in its own right. Hikers, campers, fishermen, even city dwellers who pursue none of those activities, can have enjoyment with calling, often right in their own backyards, and easily anywhere on the fringes of even the largest cities. Throughout this book the approach will be primarily that of the hunter, because the hunter fostered the science of calling and uses it most. But it is obvious that the information can be applied to immense advantage and delight by anyone who has an interest in wildlife.

It must be pointed out that calling can be a year-round activity. That is, although hunters use calls during hunting seasons, they, and others who pursue the hobby, are not *restricted* to seasonal endeavor by law. As long as you are not hunting, calling is legal at all times, except for some minor regulations in a few states. In addition, if you are not a hunter or are not

For wildlife photographers and observers, calling brings the animals in close and reduces dependence on unwieldy and costly "tele" lenses and scopes.

hunting, no license is required. Further, landowners who post their lands against hunting are usually amenable to allowing callers without guns to practice their hobby.

The subject of calling is much broader than at first may be apparent. It is not just a matter of producing *sounds* that draw an animal or bird. A duck decoy is a kind of "silent call." Used in conjunction with a call mouth-blown by the hunter, the combination creates an illusion that, properly done, pulls ducks into range. By the same token, the songbird feeder in a residential yard in the city is a variety of call. Many years ago when passenger pigeons flocked by millions over the Great Lakes region, the East and Midwest, market hunters poured brine on the ground over areas of soft earth. The pigeons needed salt, swarmed to this "bait" and were netted or shot by the thousands. All too often in past years deer poachers and deer hunters bending the law have salted a spot back in the timber, taken a stand and bagged their quarry.

Baiting of bears is legal in some states and Canadian provinces, in spring seasons, when the bears come out of hibernation and are hungry. In some states bear hunters who hunt with hounds put out baits, check them regularly for tracks, and thus are able to literally "pick out" the big bruins they want to put the dogs after — and they have a fresh track already laid. In some parts of Texas grain-filled feeders are used strategically to toll in deer and wild turkeys, and keep them where hunters can find them. In some cases stands are placed near the feeders, not exactly a sporting practice. I use the illustration to show that all such schemes are actually means of "calling" animals and birds.

3

Of course the use of sounds is, overall, the most important aspect of calling. Their use cuts across in particular all categories of game birds and game animals, from moose to bobcats, ducks to deer, quail to squirrels. The fact is that even outside the game field there is probably no living creature that could not be called, or somehow influenced to expose itself, if we but knew more than is known about how to "talk" to each.

Advances in the knowledge of ultrasonic communications will likely help biologists develop calling methods for the management of fish populations.

There has been much experimentation, for example, in listening to the voices of porpoises, and of whales, in trying to learn their "language" and its meanings. Today numerous experiments are in progress relating to sounds that fish make, and also to sounds that attract them. A few years ago a fish call was on the market that contained a small battery and a buzzer in a waterproof case. It was claimed that this implement, switched on and lowered on a string, brought fish to the sound.

Fisheries biologists have recorded ultrasonic sounds made by various fish species of the minnow family during spawning. Played back underwater, the records have brought these minnows to the sounds. It is now believed that undesirable varieties such as carp that overpopulate gamefish waters might be removed by luring them to their deaths, using recordings of their siren songs. Years ago in Louisiana diamondback terrapins were "called" by trappers who hunted them for the food market. Floating a bayou in a skiff, the market hunter tapped on the side of his boat. Any nearby turtles would immediately thrust their heads out of water, and be instantly scooped up.

Although a lot is still to be learned, a great deal already is known about calling. Interestingly, a lot of it has been unearthed, researched and developed, over a rather recent past. For example, even in the late 1950s only a scattering of sportsmen had heard anything about predator calling, and only a very few were actually practicing it. I did one of the first articles about coyote calling for a national magazine, and I'll never forget the experience that led to that story.

I was traveling across the U.S. and had paused in Laredo, Texas, where I met local game warden Whit Whitenton. We went driving on his beat, and he asked if I'd ever heard of a coyote being called up with a call that sounded like an injured rabbit. I told him not to put too much stock in those tales — which shows how comparatively recently coyote calling knowledge has been dispersed. Whit chuckled, stopped his car on a ranch trail, produced a call from his pocket, one of the first such calls on the market. At that time of course all predators were naive. They'd not had experience with man-blown calls, as they have today. He stood right beside the car and blew the call. And in a couple of minutes *four* big coyotes bounded out of various places in the brush and raced straight at us. I simply could not believe it.

I immediately started learning to call coyotes, foxes, and bobcats. Later when we went to live in Texas I learned about "rattling up" buck deer during the rut by banging a pair of antlers together. I hadn't put much stock in that, either, until Charlie Schreiner, owner of the well-known YO Ranch, sat me down in a thicket and brought a wild-eyed buck on the run almost into the thicket with us. Several years ago, while producing a TV film for one of the firearms firms, I rattled up fifty-two whitetail bucks in ten days!

Calling, regardless of the size of the game, is indeed a sensational outdoor experience. Imagine, for instance, dressing in camouflage suit and headnet, sitting beneath a tree and working a squirrel call. A gray squirrel answers, and over a period of a few minutes comes perhaps a full hundred yards to sit above you, chattering. Some hobby callers learn to make mouth sounds — without the aid of a mechanical call — so authentic that they can mesmerize birds and animals. I sat in a boat on Lake

While guiding for the author, Rex Grady called-up this owl by means of mouth sounds that mimicked the owl's mating call.

Taneycomo in Missouri one spring and watched my guide, Rex Grady, fetch a horned owl out of the bordering woods this way. He spotted the owl, mimicked owl mating calls, got a reply, and the big bird came to perch above us. Another, hearing the commotion, presently appeared, yammering at the first. Then Grady started crow calling, also just by mouth sounds, and brought crows, which spotted the owls — which crows despise — and the birds made a terrible din.

These are just a few offhand examples of what calling is all about, and how varied it can be. One facet of the subject is even a kind of "reverse" approach. This is when a call is used to deliberately frighten a bird or animal, to make a game bird, for example, sit tight instead of running, so a hunting dog can point it. Or, the call is used to frighten instead of intrigue an animal into exposing itself. As an example, a coyote call blown loudly and wildly will often flush whitetail deer from dense thickets.

Although hearing is the chief sense appealed to in calling, there are others. Sight plays a part occasionally, as with decoys. But there are other aspects of sight appeal. Old-time duck hunters once used "tolling dogs" trained to run up and down a beach in sight of ducks out of range offshore. The ducks, becoming *curious*, swam into range. Antelope and caribou can be brought in close by such ridiculous procedures as lying down and waving your hat. Again the appeal is to curiosity. Scent also has a place in

Seemingly a contradiction of terms, "silent calls" such as visible decoys and lures can greatly influence a caller's success.

Here a hunter begins flying a bird-like kite over a spread of decoys to help fool migrating snow geese.

calling. Scents can be used to bring animals close, as by the use of urine, for example, by bobcat trappers. Scents are also used not to appeal directly to the quarry but as a means of masking human odor.

Many hearing-sight combinations are useful. Dead crows or magpies tossed into the air while a call is blown by the hidden caller bring more of those species to the scene. Goose hunters sometimes not only put out decoys on feedings grounds, but hang fluttering newspapers on strings from stakes, and even put up goose-facsimile kites, all to add to the illusion while the call is blown.

Calls appeal to several basic emotions of wildlife. Predator calls intimate that an easy kill is at hand. Hunger brings the animal to the call, or sometimes greed lures it there. In some studies, coyotes have been cut open and found to have as many as ten pack rats in the stomach, yet the animal had raced to a call, eager to eat more. We've already noted the appeal to curiosity in some instances. Sex—the mating urge—figures in several calling endeavors: a wild gobbler comes to "hen talk" in spring; rattling deer antlers simulates bucks fighting over a doe; the baleful bawl of a moose cow, ready to be bred, brings in the bull.

When deer antlers are rattled they arouse anger as well as the mating urge. The desire to do battle urges the buck to move in. Beating of brush in moose country arouses a listening bull in rut to rush toward the sound, intent on bracing a competitor. Desire for companionship and safety, as well as for food, brings waterfowl to decoys and call. We've already noted the occasional need for the caller to appeal to fear.

Animal and bird calling, in clever but by current standards rather rudimentary ways, was to early peoples a serious part of making a living. Indians rapped on a canoe to bring curious beaver near. Others "squeaked up" muskrats to be taken for both food and fur. Draped in a buffalo hide, one Indian acted as toller to lure buffalo into ambush. Indians imitated the low bleat of a deer fawn to lure the doe out to see what was wrong. Indians also knew how to imitate the spring mating hoot of big blue grouse in high forests. Getting an answer, they could then stalk the perched bird. An imitated owl hoot on a clear dawn during spring breeding season caused turkey toms to gobble. In this manner Indians located the big birds. Banging a stick against a tree at dawn also sometimes brought a startled gobble out of a listening tom. Indian hunting knowledge has been passed along, and is still used today.

Primitive peoples devised and practiced many elaborate ruses to outwit wildlife. One such was donning a hat of reeds woven in the shape of a duck; then with a breathing reed held in his mouth and swimming along the surface of the water, the hunter could glide into a flock of ducks and seize several by the feet. It was common also for an Indian to dress in a wolf skin and crawl near a buffalo herd, thus pushing the herd toward ambush. Indians also used wolfskin dress so that they might sit to observe the movements of various game animals.

Primitives knew much about scents, too. They burned, or smoked, various plants, either to cover up their own odor or as an attraction to the quarry. Some Indians believed the scent of burning dry wild aster imitated the scent from the hoof gland of deer. Beaver castor, mink and weasel scent, skunk scent, mountain lion urine—all were used either as "bait" to bring animals near, or else to kill or overpower human scent.

Many a pioneer American learned, and passed down, the art of early tribal calling customs. The wingbone of a turkey was (and sometimes still is) fashioned into a gobbler call. Pintail ducks were "whistled down" by mouth imitation of their lilting call. The squeak of a mouse, just as I imitated it for my boys by "kissing" my palm, brought foxes on the run centuries ago. Alligators were located by imitating a bellowing bull and getting a replying

These alligators came to within a few feet of the author after he tossed clumps of mud into the water to simulate sounds of splashing fish.

challenge. Or, clods of mud or small sticks were tossed into a pond and alligators, thinking the sound was splashing fish, came to investigate. I have in fact accomplished this myself. Sitting in camouflage suit in shade on a pond bank, I brought five alligators, all about four feet long, to within a few yards.

These myriad ruses are, in total, what calling is all about. For the hunter, the lore is just possibly the most important to success of all hunting knowledge. To the nonhunter, it can furnish some of the most memorable, dramatic and intriguing of all outdoor experiences.

2

Sounds and Signals of Wildlife

ANIMALS AND BIRDS do have languages. Man has learned the basics of some of them. Obviously these languages are not as intricate as those humans have devised. The difference between thinking man and instinctive animals is that while man may need extremely involved systems of expression, animals do not.

Nonetheless, undoubtedly many wildlife languages are far more complicated than we imagine. In the foregoing chapter I mentioned studies of communication among porpoises. This is an excellent example. Presumably—from what is known at this stage—their communication is quite intricate and broad in scope. However, generally speaking, birds and animals do not require nor possess abilities beyond indicating the most fundamental feelings: hunger; discomfort or pain; fright; curiosity; the sex urge; and contentment or comfort, that is, a sense of well being and safety. Before a caller can possibly aspire to full-blown success, he certainly must study and be aware of the meanings of wildlife language. It is blatantly obvious that a sound made by the caller that represents a fear or anxiety sound in the language of his quarry will only cause the creature to hide, flee, or at least be alerted and suspicious.

I remember with amusement taking two men from Detroit, Michigan, out into the thornbrush and cactus of southern Texas, to try to call up a coyote for them. They had never seen this done, and knew nothing whatever about coyotes. So errors in judgment were understandable, but theirs were also comic.

We quietly took up a stand where we could see a broad saladillo flat surrounded by brush. I began blowing the call. Almost instantly a group of at least two or three coyotes began to howl, bark and yodel. It is a wild and thrilling sound, I'll admit. Both gentlemen hit the ground with guns ready, wild eyed, finding this incredible.

12

One hissed at the other, "Don't move a muscle! Here they come!"

He hadn't seen anything. It just seemed logical to him that we'd got an instant rise out of the critters and that they were about to charge in after an easy meal — maybe us. The correct interpretation of their sounds, however, was derision. I will admit that a lot is still to be learned about why coyotes at times wail and bark back at a caller. Perhaps they've seen or scented him. But when they do, you can just bet they're saying: "You might as well quit that foolishness because we're not going to pay any attention." This is a classic example of the fact that callers must be familiar with wildlife language.

Language of contentment or well being is important simply because a caller who recognizes it is being told that he has not been discovered, that the quarry is not suspicious or afraid. It is not necessary to be able to translate every syllable of such "talk." As an illustration, I think of listening to mockingbirds in my own yard. I've heard one sing away for fifteen minutes, switching every few musical bars to another scrap of ditty, and never once repeating itself. This is an amazing performance. Naturally I don't know if each new excerpt was a new and different statement. Only another mockingbird could tell. But the fact is, this was a contented, unsuspicious bird. My point is that what we vitally need to know is the basics.

Bull elk bugle only during the rut. It is useless to try to call them at other times.

It is very important to listen closely to animal and bird sounds, so that you memorize precisely the tones they use, the pitch and inflection of each "sentence." In addition, many birds call in a series, a series of three, four, six or more of the same note or phrase repeated, then a pause. It is even advantageous to check on how long the usual interval is between calls. These will differ of course, among individual birds and animals, but there is among members of any species a general pattern. By paying attention, the caller learns to call sparingly, or with greater frequency as the need may be.

You will understand as these chapters proceed that some sounds of wildlife are seasonal. Bull elk bugle, for example, only during the rutting season in fall. Thus it would be useless to try bugling up a bull with your call, say, in June. Some sounds of nature are produced most commonly and regularly at specific times of day—the gobbling of turkeys early in the morning, the crowing of cock pheasants early and late in the day. Further, in some cases sounds are made at predictable places. That is, crows congregate noisily at the roosting site late in the afternoon, but do not utilize it during the day. Doves sit on dead snags and coo morning and afternoon, but are quieter at their roost sites, and while resting at midday.

Nonhunters learning to call are advised to scout for signs such as tracks and droppings, which can indicate species, size, quantity, proximity, and travel habits. A bobcat made these tracks.

In my anecdote about my boys and the fox, I mentioned having seen fox tracks on our ranch. If you are to be a successful caller, obviously you have to operate where the animal or bird is that you intend to call. So, do some studying in animal and bird books — a book of tracks is a good source also — about ranges of varied species, the terrain they prefer, what each eats. And then be constantly alert for various signs: tracks, droppings, signs of feeding, availability of water and signs near water indicating it is being used. Most hunters are aware of animal signs, but nonhunters may need this reminder.

By always being alert for signs, you can also judge abundance. To be sure, a few deer can leave a lot of tracks. But a few deer *tracks* usually mean a very sparse population. Coyotes and foxes commonly follow ranch trails, old roads, and animal trails, leaving tracks and droppings that are easily spotted. If you find none, or many, in such places, you have a good idea of the quality of that particular range.

Something that can be immensely helpful is listening to records of actual recordings of bird and animal sounds. Some are available, from call makers, for example. I once had a series of small records that were made up into a book and offered by the National Geographic Society, with calls of numerous shore and water birds on them. Recordings of actual calling, done by expert callers, are also available and these are most helpful to play and study. If you have opportunity to visit game farms, preserves, and even on occasion some zoo, you can learn much about bird and animal talk. I gained a lot of knowledge one time from listening to wild turkeys that were held in a pen on a ranch I visited.

Bear in mind, however, that wildlife language is by no means all vocal. Some animals, and birds, too, are not very vocal at all. Some so far as is known make only a few sounds. But there are many physical *signals* that form a kind of "body language" just as among humans. A quail or turkey observed at a distance dusting in a trail is plainly saying all is well. A mule deer standing on a hillside on a warm day and switching its big ears incessantly is being bothered only by some flying insect pests. But when its ears come up to full alert and it turns to stare toward your hiding place, you know by this body language that it is alerted.

Those are of course quite obvious examples. Others require more careful study and appraisal. Whitetail deer offer a classic example. They are nervous, jittery animals. They have a whole basic language involved just with motions and stance of the tail. Observe a feeding doe. Her head stays down only for a few seconds. Then she jerks it erect, looks around intently. Sometimes she'll stare for a seemingly endless interval. Don't move even an eyelid during this time. Her tail is down so far. Keep your eye on her tail. Eventually, if she is not suspicious or alarmed, she'll give a little switch of the tail. That's an "all clear" signal. Down goes her head and she begins eating again.

When a whitetail buck runs or even walks with tail straight out during the fall, he's probably in rut and following a doe.

If, while staring, she begins to raise the tail, not to horizontal but at least some, she is uneasy. She will probably move her head from side to side, ears cocked. This movement is her attempt to see a suspicious image better. Her eyes are not as good as yours on immobile objects, but are fantastically sharp to the slightest movement. Deer are color blind. Their world is made up of black, white, and intermediate shades of gray. If she lowers the tail and switches it, things are okay. But if she stamps her foot, not so good.

Now the tail is raised to full horizontal. She is highly suspicious, and in all probability she is going to leave. If she does lower it, she may not switch it "all clear" because now she is totally uneasy. She may drift away, not terrified, but just listening to her intuition. If while her tail is horizontal it suddenly moves a bit higher and over to one side, she is as good as long gone. When she raises the tail straight up in a flag, she has either already wheeled and plunged away or will in a second. As she bounds off, tail high and waving back and forth, she's saying good-bye.

Occasionally a whitetail deer will be seen to trot or run off with tail down. Generally this means one of two things: the deer is sick or wounded, or it doesn't believe it has been seen but has had time to settle down. Immediate pursuit or calling would not be wise. Of course bucks and does both use the same tail signals. During the rut, incidentally, you may occasionally see a whitetail buck running with its tail held out straight behind. If you are able to observe closely with a binocular, you'll probably see that its mouth is open. This is not a frightened deer. It is chasing a doe. There's a good possibility you can rattle antlers and bring it around.

The foregoing gives you an idea of the intricacies of wildlife language. An entire book undoubtedly could be written about it. I can give only rudiments here, but at least the most important ones in relation to calling. However, I would urge every reader to diligently observe any creature in which he is interested, as a hunter, a photographer, or hobbyist. Days spent hiking or in blinds watching birds and animals, without calling, are not only interesting and pleasant but will pay off with high profit when you do use your calls.

As another example among deer, mule deer are far more placid animals than are whitetails. But they, too, use a body language of their own. A mule deer that has become suspicious but not really frightened may start to strut away slowly, left front leg stepping, then right, and the head meanwhile bobbing back and forth the long way of its body. It acts almost embarrassed. A bigger dose of suspicion will cause the deer to hop away with a bouncing, comical gait. It bends its legs and hops almost straight up, comes down on all fours, bounces again. After a short distance it stops and looks back. But if the deer is really spooked, believe me it can bound away taking fifteen or twenty feet at a time. Yet this species of deer well may haul up and stand on a ridgetop to look back again. And it may then drift over the other side and start feeding again, unconcerned. Conversely, a whitetail will run over the next four ridges without stopping. All this is deer "language."

Body language varies greatly between whitetails and mule deer. But when either species brings its ears to full alert and aims them in your direction, as this mule deer is doing, you'll be lucky to go unidentified for long.

Deer are among the least vocal of animals. The most common sound they make, especially whitetails, is a snort, or "whistle," as air is blown forcibly out through the nostrils. This is an alarm signal. It certainly should not be used by a caller, unless he wishes to frighten deer. Many hunters have learned to imitate the sound well by mouth, and use it to spook deer out of canyons and thickets, when making a drive or standing to watch flight exits. An advantage of using it this way is that hidden deer may sneak out, not bolting full tilt as they would if they heard a man yelling.

In summer, fawns at times utter a low bleat. Sometimes this bleat is a sound of fear. At others it is obviously just a quest to be reassured by the doe. Deer will react positively to this sound. This bleat is not common as a rule during deer seasons in fall. I have heard it only a couple of times in many years of hunting. However, deer are conditioned to react, and many times will.

Bucks occasionally utter a rather loud, abrupt *blatt*, like an explosive *bah*. This sound is usually associated with the rut, and is uttered now and then as two bucks fight. It is not a common forest sound, but you should be aware of it to interpret what it is, if and when it is heard; for you may be able to rattle up such a buck. A buck chasing a doe will also now and then utter a guttural grunt, in a short series. This is made with the mouth either closed or only partially open: *Uhh--uhh-uhh*. It is not a sound commonly used by callers, but it definitely is one you should recognize. Learn to mimic it by mouth, and you may cause a buck making it to have a look. In general mule deer are a bit less vocal and less aggressive than whitetails.

Many kinds of wildlife emit only a few vocal sounds. This fawn may bleat quietly when hungry, but it will otherwise remain silent, except when frightened.

An alarmed antelope will usually flare its white rump patch. This signals others in the herd that something is amiss.

Antelope are no more vocal than deer. The one most important signal they flash is raising the white rump hairs into a broad, flashing puff of white by use of specialized muscles along the rump. This is an alarm signal. Because antelope are gregarious animals, consorting in bands large or small, undoubtedly this reaction to danger is used to signal an alert to others of the group.

If you observe the javelina of the Southwest closely, you will note that it has poor eyesight but a good sense of smell. A band may potter about, grunting, the young squealing. But with suspicion aroused, adults will often strain the head and nose as high into the air as possible. These animals are built low to the ground, and the upraised nose indicates that they are trying to pick up scent. If javelina do catch a suspicious scent or if they hear or see something that makes them uneasy, their long neck bristles raise, making a javelina of forty pounds look to a tyro hunter as if it weighed two hundred. If alarm heightens, the animals clack and pop their teeth together, bluffing danger. When they flee, or walk away, bristles surrounding the musk sack high on the rump open flowerlike and emit musk. Sudden alarm and flight is accompanied by a series of chuffing, grunting sounds.

The most important elk sound is the bugling of the bulls during rut. An astute hunter will listen to each voice closely. It is easy to distinguish young (spike) bulls by their high, thin, reedy bugles. Mature bulls give deep, wracking, coughing grunts and literally scream with very rough-edged tones.

The sounds made by smaller animals, and their reactions to catching human scent, or suddenly becoming suspicious are also important to know, and sometimes quite dramatic. A fox may come running in when you call at night, then suddenly stand some distance away and growl with unbelievable volume and viciousness. A caller unaccustomed to this sound would think an animal six times as large had come to his call. The fox, puzzled, uncertain and suspicious, is trying to frighten whatever made that calling sound into exposure. It may not run away for some time, but it is not likely to come closer.

Bobcats are unpredictable. When suspicious they may just sit on their haunches at a distance and stare in your direction.

Bobcats are enigmas to tyro callers. They seldom rush in. But they have a habit, when suspicious, of sitting on their haunches and staring. A cat that has even seen a caller, or scented him, may do this and finally retire without coming closer or within possible range. Conversely, the crafty coyote that so much as crosses a fresh human track when coming to a call will turn tail and race away.

Birds in general are more vocal than mammals. Learn to properly interpret their talk. Pheasant cocks crow at dawn and dusk. This is an all-is-well sound. But the loud cackle uttered by a flushing cock pheasant is an all-out alarm. Quail have a variety of calls, the "bob-white" call, the reedy crowing of scaled and Gambel's and other quail. They also use alarm calls and, because they are covey birds, "get-back-together" calls after they've become separated. The congenial *perk, perk, perk* and several other sounds made by feeding wild turkeys tell you they are feeling safe and content. If you flush a flock and scatter the individuals, the questing calls they begin a few minutes later are "get-together" appeals. Their flock instinct has conditioned them to do this. But if you are calling a wily tom and have him coming to you, then suddenly he bursts out with an explosive *Putt!* – he's long gone.

An expert crow caller can distinguish among flock calls, anger calls, and alarm calls. Crows are exceedingly vocal. So are waterfowl. They utter feeding calls, assurance calls, and they have numerous and sometimes very low-decibel danger calls. Many times I've hunkered in a feeding field near a set of goose decoys and listened to the thrilling *Kerwonk, kerwonk* of snows and blues sweeping across toward the spread. Then, perhaps lying flat on my back, I watch an old gander somewhere up front cock his neck from side to side. He gives a low-toned kind of grunt, very quiet compared to the former cries of the flock. And he shifts course almost imperceptibly. He's saying to the others, "Don't go down there!" And the flock veers far out of range.

Each species of bird and animal has also what may be termed an "approach distance." This means that a given variety will allow the approach of man (danger) just so close and no closer. This distance differs greatly and among species. And it is also directly proportional to the amount of harassment the species has endured. Coyotes that have been called several times and have seen the caller are not inclined to come close, and may not respond at all. A flock of geese may feed in a field where cars pass close by constantly on an interstate. But a hunter walking across the field can move to only a range the geese judge far enough.

Turkeys are flocking birds. They talk as they feed and emit a get-together call after they've been flushed or scattered.

Deer, antelope, squirrels, quail—every variety of wildlife has its "approach distance." No one can tell you in yards what each is. As noted, these distances will differ with how "wild" human disturbances have made the species in that location. You can learn approach distances in your area through acute observation. They often have vital bearing on the success of your calling.

In addition, reaction, or lack of it, to calling is directly proportional to how much calling has been done in the vicinity and how expert the caller is. Ducks called several times and shot at are extremely wary. Young geese just coming to wintering grounds are naive. Foxes called and shot at, or those that have seen the caller and know they were fooled, become shy.

Most species of birds at rest, on the ground or in trees, have a universal alarm signal. It is a matter of stretching the neck and thrusting the head up. Any quail, pheasant, goose, duck that is feeding or resting and suddenly thrusts its head upward as far as its neck will reach is telling you plainly that it is extremely alarmed, and wary.

Later, in the chapters about calling individual species, we will discuss in more detail some of the phenomena mentioned in this chapter. It has been my intent here simply to impress you with the importance of listening to and observing diligently any creature you wish to attempt to call. Every movement each makes, every sound uttered, every reaction to you or to other animals has meaning. Proper interpretation and translation of these meanings will take you a big step along the way toward becoming an expert caller.

3

The Art of Concealment

NOT ALL, but most, calling requires that the caller conceal himself in some manner from his quarry. The exceptions occur when using a call to flush some bird or animal into movement. Then it makes no difference whether or not the caller is hiding. But when calling is done to *attract* wildlife, regardless of the emotion appealed to, then the caller must be well hidden or camouflaged. Once the caller has gained the attention of a bird or animal, it will be looking toward, and probably moving toward, the caller's position. Because of the keen senses of all wildlife, concealment is an art in its own right.

Further, you've not only called general attention to your position, but in most instances you have unalterably riveted the creature's gaze and alerted its senses. The buck coming to rattled antlers may be expecting to see two other bucks fighting. But you can bet he will be totally alert. The elk moving toward your "whistle" during bugling season will be looking for another bull perhaps with a harem. He may be startled and confused when or if he spots the caller—but not for long. A coyote racing to that injured rabbit squall is after an easy meal. This is an extremely sensitive animal. It can precisely pinpoint the spot from whence the sound emanated, even from a distance. And, it is totally intent on moving to that exact place. If anything suddenly seems not to look right, the coyote will flee in a flash. Thus it is obvious that concealment must be craftily accomplished.

BASICS OF CAMOUFLAGE

The caller who is careless about his camouflage will never be very successful.

First of all, one has to understand that "camouflage" doesn't necessarily mean simply pulling on a modern camouflage suit. The art of concealment is many-faceted. Going back to our earlier chapters, the In-

23

dian with the reed "duck" on his head and swimming underwater is utilizing a kind of camouflage. The Indian dressed in a wolf skin or buffalo hide is doing likewise. This variety of camouflage is a masquerade. Some very clever ruses fall into this category.

I remember one time hunting ducks on a shallow pond across the center of which ran a barbed wire fence. The ducks would not come near shore. But they did trade back and forth in flight to various areas of the pond, and I observed that a high percentage of them passed over the cross fence about midway. I waded out to the fence, wearing hip boots and a drab rain parka. I hunched against a post and kept my shotgun in a perpendicular position along the post. Some birds shied off because I looked perhaps like too large a post. But enough were fooled so that I collected a limit.

This trick was a joining of two types of camouflage—pretending to be something I wasn't, and using a part of the familiar landscape. The most common form of camouflage—and very effective when properly done—falls into this broad category. You size up the area where you will be operating and select specific features in it that either will hide you or break up your outline. Stepping into the middle of a small mott of brush in an otherwise rather open terrain, and hunkering there, is a natural. But you must remember to wear clothing that matches. A white shirt stuck into a dark patch of brush is hardly good for hiding.

Always bear in mind that animals and birds living in a given area are intimately familiar with every stick, stone, bush and tree. If you

Here the author in full camouflage tricks ducks by appearing to be part of a fence post.

Although it's best to wear camouflage, many animals are color blind. Thus if parts of you don't contrast markedly with your surroundings and you remain immobile, you can call animals up close without being seen. Here rocks allow good hiding.

came home after being away several days you'd be certain to notice a scrap of paper lying in your driveway or a tin can on your lawn. This is your home and you are completely familiar with it. The slightest item out of order calls attention. Animals are even more observant because they must live by their wits and with incessant, surrounding dangers. Thus the obvious white shirt, or any slight difference in the landscape, is likely, at the very least, to draw attention. Further, referring momentarily to that patch of brush in an open area, all wildlife knows instinctively that such a spot is a perfect hiding place for danger, as well as for forage. Animals will look such spots over carefully as a matter of course.

Classic examples of utilizing landscape features and becoming a part of them were the practices of waterfowl hunters years ago. A market hunter walked along a lakeshore, let's say, and saw a scattering of sticks and small drift logs with wisps of marsh grass growing among the jumble. He sprawled there beside a log, not with legs straight but limply cocked at angles, and arms likewise. His head was perhaps propped against the log but not high above ground, and a bunch of leaning marsh grass shaded his face. He could see through the grass, but his face would not show. His outlines were broken up.

25

He had attended to masking any shiny places on his gun. The metal was well blued and probably rusty to boot. And he laid the gun down into the grass as if it were another stick. An upright barrel would not have looked natural to flying birds and might have cast an unnatural shadow.

There are important lessons to be learned from such practices. You must always think in terms of trying to become a part of the scenery, but not a *new* or *unnatural* part. If you have to contrive somehow because there is little cover, and you must be a "bulge" or "lump" of some sort, try to be one that looks natural.

Once you've riveted an animal's attention with a call, it's best to be well concealed. A camo net hides your face from your quarry. It also helps protect against pesky insects, making the wait more comfortable.

I think again of waterfowl hunting. One time I was determined to get a couple of geese that were using a very small pond right out in an open pasture. There were a few bunches of big bluestem grass scattered sparsely here and there. A ranch road ran past the little waterhole. It was the only one for some miles, and I had a hunch that geese flushed from here would return. I had a friend drive past the pond, keeping it on the driver's side. As the vehicle approached, the geese flew. I rolled out the other side as the driver slowed, and I dropped flat. As the birds disappeared, I crawled over into the field but within gun range of the pond. I had on camo clothing that matched the bunch grass. I sat down and hunched over trying to look like one of the clumps, gun across my lap. In half an hour the geese came back, calling, circling the pond. On the third circle they dropped low, set their wings. I could hear the swish of gliding wings right over me. I tagged a pair for the pot, practically off the end of the gun barrel.

Undoubtedly the first lesson to be learned in hiding is that among all wild creatures there is nothing more terrifying or distasteful than a look at a human face. Many a deer, elk, duck, goose, squirrel and other game has fled prematurely because it caught a glimpse of this anathema. Always select your hiding spot and contrive your cover and camouflage so that your face is at the very least in deep shadow, or else covered up. Camouflage headnets should be a part of every caller's equipment. A full headnet is, admittedly, hard to see through for some, and difficult to sight either camera or gun through. But you can cut eyeholes in such a net. Some already have them. One brilliant idea is a mask type of net that is hung on a device like a pair of lensless glasses. The bows fit over one's ears and the mask hangs down from them to cover all of the face except the eyes. The forehead is covered by the camouflage cap brim.

Archers commonly blacken their faces. There are creams and stick paste made especially for this. I've seen many an old-time turkey hunter cut a green leafy branch in spring and sit back against a big tree bole to work his call, with the sharpened end of the branch stuck into the ground so that the leaves concealed his face. The play of light and shadow breaks up the outline and obscures the human face.

Hands are almost as bad a giveaway as the face, chiefly because they may be busy operating a call, or, in the case of most people, always moving to some degree. A bird or animal may have no idea what the flesh-colored flapping thing is, but it doesn't belong in the scene, that's certain. If your hands are uncovered, keep them in your lap, under a fold of jacket, behind cover, or somehow out of sight. The easy modern way is to buy, and wear, camouflage gloves. There are very thin net types available for warm weather. You can easily operate call, gun, camera while wearing them. There are heavier ones on the market for colder weather.

CONCEALING YOUR MOVEMENTS

I've often thought that callers, whether with camera, gun, bow or binocular, should actually practice at odd moments complete immobility. Just for fun, sometime sit down on the ground by a tree in your yard and see how long you can remain completely motionless. No head movement. No hitching around, scratching, twiddling fingers, moving feet or legs. You will quickly discover that total immobility is a unique experience. Few persons are capable of it, without full concentration, for any extended period.

Given the choice, the hunter blends better with his surroundings when sitting against a tree rather than kneeling beside it. This also provides a more comfortable wait and increases the chances that an animal may approach from the rear and enter the field of view.

Immobility is not accomplished by being tense. Quite the opposite, it requires utter relaxation. While letting all muscles of your arms, legs and body relax, try the trick of concentrating on keeping your *tongue from touching your teeth,* and letting *it* wholly relax. Keep eyes alert and looking but let the lid muscles relax and concentrate on this also. Curiously, the emphasis on tongue and eyelids will have a surprising effect upon other muscles.

I must point out that any movements a caller makes should be in extremely slow motion. Actually this is a fact well known to—but not always observed by—hunters. Let us suppose you are well set on a calling stand. You raise a call to your lips, or however it is operated. The first time you do this, the *way* it is done is by no means as important as from there on. For all you know, your *first* call has swiveled animal eyes to the spot. When you lower the call from your mouth—if you do—move your hands very slowly and with no stops and starts. If you must turn your head to look at something, do it in slow motion. If you must change positions, ditto. I have sat many times with deer within a few yards of me, unable to catch scent, and been able to raise and lower a long-lens camera, bulky indeed, without running them off, because I did it in an extremely slow, but *steady,* motion.

Next, when you have selected a stand, before you make the first call, be absolutely certain you are comfortable. Not for ten minutes, but indefinitely. You should not make a lot of noise getting comfortable. Plan ahead. Select a stand — you might even do this and arrange it some days before you start calling — and then when you sit or stand at or in it, have it so arranged that your physical comfort will not require a lot of hitching and hunching, rising and sitting back down. A small stone under your backside will grow to become a boulder in fifteen minutes. A twig poking you in the neck will be a saber in twenty. Arrange to be totally relaxed. You may need to move your legs, or arms, but make your setup so this can be accomplished unobtrusively. The point is, you might sit and call for half an hour. Then, discouraged, you'll move around — and that is the exact second when Mr. Bobcat, or Mr. Big Bull Elk, appears.

The comfort concept has another dimension: noise. Whether you stand or sit, or lie flat, you are going to go through some movements over a period of minutes, or an hour or more. No human can remain as immobile over such an extended period of time as can varied wildlife species. When you select a site for standing or sitting, look for twigs or dry sticks beneath your boots. They snap or crackle when you are at the most crucial stage, and slightly move your feet. Are there twigs or branches catching your headnet from behind or at the side, or hooking a jacket pocket?

I know a gentleman who bugled up an enormous bull elk and, trying to raise his rifle, discovered an Achilles Heel had tethered him — a small branch was hooked into his camo pocket and inhibited his rifle movement. I know another caller who had a bobcat within mere feet, and he wanted one badly for a rug. But, alas, leaning back into a persimmon bush, which had exasperatingly stiff, tough twigs, he had caught one in his headnet. He jerked forward, it jerked back — and the cat was long gone.

CHOOSING A STAND

Most callers will be operating in territory to which they will return numerous times. That is, they'll be using calls near home. Be sure to case your bailiwick thoroughly beforehand. Where are the best places in it for you to hide? Are they locations that will give you a proper view? Will the sound of the call carry as it should from them? I realize that different types of sites will be applicable to different varieties of quarry, but consider all the angles in selecting places from which to call.

Certainly you should not select a stand atop a ridge where you are skylighted from below. And if you'll have reason to try calling anything from geese to foxes out in the open, as on a plowed field, you'll have to contrive a pit or blind of some sort and then stay away from it long enough to let resident wildlife get used to it, till it has become a part of the landscape to them. Most creatures on the ground will come to your call not across wide openings, but via routes that offer *them* concealment.

Since incoming water-fowl will land into the wind, set out your decoys in relation to your blind accordingly.

In that regard, I have long been impressed by the fact that, when rattling whitetail bucks, one may come into a small woodland opening where I have set up. He may appear in the edge of the opening, then move out a few feet into the open, but not very far. If there is a single bush or tree between him and my hiding place, the buck will circle behind that bit of cover to peer out. Thus, always try to select calling stands *so you offer the animal its "stalking cover."* This helps allay its timidity. Your target can be confident that it has not been seen by "whatever is making that sound."

If you will be calling any of the predators, or deer, for example, you will need to have selected several sites. You should try for twenty minutes to half an hour at one spot. No action. You must move. If you move only a short distance—a few yards let's say—you'll only confuse any listening animals or arouse their suspicion. The plan should be to move far enough so that if animals resident to that first area have heard you, you will be out of their hearing for the next try, and will be working on a fresh population. This distance will differ with calling conditions (weather) and with the species in question. Two hundred yards might be far enough when rattling antlers for deer in heavy brush. A half mile or a mile may be necessary when calling coyotes.

30

This brings us to the problem of your movement to the calling stand, whether it is your approach to the first and only spot or movement from site to site. If you approach in the open, you may alert every creature to your presence. Calling then is useless. An animal that has seen a man, and then hears a call, will seldom pay any attention. Thus, lay out your routes to the site or between sites to give you every chance of complete concealment.

YOUR SCENT AND THE WIND

I've purposely not mentioned breeze direction until now, to concentrate on hiding from the *eyes* of wildlife. But obviously outwitting an animal's awesomely keen sense of smell is of utmost importance. It is even more important than remaining unseen, for occasionally an animal may glimpse you as you move but not be unduly disturbed unless it gets a whiff of human scent.

In moving to a stand, check direction of air movement very meticulously. Windy, gusty days are seldom good calling days anyway. On what you consider still days, test for a breeze anyway by filtering dust or bits of dead grass from your fingers high above ground. Then plan your site approach to keep the air movement always in your favor. Move into the breeze, but, take a stand so that you can see around you in at least a 180 degree arc, and preferably more. The reason for this is, having moved upwind, you have allowed your scent to drift behind you. Given a steady breeze direction, you have alerted creatures behind you, but not necessarily those off at the sides. Thus you may get action from either side or from upwind.

Virtually without fail, all animals will *circle* a caller to "get the wind on the call site." This is a natural hunting instinct for predators, and a natural move for any animal that depends upon a keen sense of smell to home in on any target area. This means that you must be well concealed from the sides as well as the front, and that you must watch with constant alertness for animal movement anywhere along the arc.

Consider also that if you have pre-selected your calling stands in a given tract, you must plot which ones will be good on an east wind, which on a west wind, and so on. Otherwise you waste your time and educate your prey. Seldom will you find a spot that will do regardless of wind direction. Know also which way roads or trails run in the area. It is always best, if possible, to move along a trail rather than cut across game cover. You can move more quietly, and you are not invading the resting or hunting or feeding areas of your targets. If you move on a north-south trail, and the wind is from the west, your scent will have swept much country on the east side. So pay little attention to the east. Concentrate on the west side.

Whenever it is feasible, move to your site or between sites in a *vehicle*. Wildlife is not as uneasy about passing vehicles as passing humans on foot.

Further, your scent can be closed inside. Leave the car some distance from the stand, in a gully or in brush where animals won't see it. Get out quietly. Don't slam doors. Move with stealth to the scene of operations.

Always, when calling any creature, bird or animal, unless wind direction or time of day forbids it, place yourself in shade, and with the sun at your back. Shade, even that of a small leafless bush, breaks up your outline. But probably more important, if you are looking down-sun—away from the sun—you are forcing animals or birds to look into the sun. This is just as difficult for them, especially when the sun is at a low angle, as it is for you. Give yourself every advantage.

In bird calling, of course, scent is not important. Sense of smell is not well developed in them. Wind direction therefore makes little difference. When calling waterfowl, regardless of sun and other considerations, everything is just reversed. Waterfowl must land *into* the wind. Thus your site must be selected and decoys set out so you are watching downwind. There are exceptions. A gentle air movement doesn't concern the birds to any great degree and they may land from any direction. But on a modest to stiff breeze they will wheel around and come into the wind to your call and decoys.

If you learn to pay close attention to the problems of terrain and stand selection in your home area or a familiar region, you will discover that it is then easy to go to a new place, perhaps in a distant state, where everything is changed, and still quickly size up what you must do. Desert and plain have features that can be translated to fit what you have already learned, let's say from operating in a forested area. The basic rules will always apply.

This hunter has just stepped out from behind Spanish bayonet to shoot. He effectively kept the sun in the deer's eyes.

MASKING YOUR SCENT

In later chapters about individual species we will discuss in more detail the scents that you can use. But a few generalities are in order here because certain scents available in the stores, or even those that a caller can put together himself, are often useful tools related to hiding and camouflage. Some scents are used to lure animals. But the ones related to our immediate subject are those that either create an illusion that an animal of the same species you are calling has been here, or is here, or else they mask or cover the man smell.

One fall while experimenting with rattling buck whitetails, two of us cut the musk glands from the hind legs of several deer that hunters had brought in. We carried these in a jar, hung them on bushes near us as we rattled. I cannot say positively that they were a help, but they certainly didn't do any harm, and there is the chance that their strong odor added to the illusion because a buck came to the sound of the rattled antlers. Sometimes predator callers use scents based on urine from the animal being called. Fox urine scents, coyote, bobcat and others are available. These may not in all cases actually draw the animals, but they do assist in covering the scent of the caller and of adding to the illusion.

Historically, Indians and other primitive peoples considered scents extremely important. Musk glands, bladders full of urine, gall bladders, were taken from all animals killed and used presumably in attempts to attract others of their kind. One practice hardly suitable to today's callers I suspect was that of using fresh manure to rub on the body or clothing. Buffalo dung or other animal droppings covered up the human scent and made the hunter smell like the game he pursued. Commonly the fat of animals was rendered and the oil rubbed on the hunter's body. Or, he wore the hide of a fresh-killed animal for several days before a hunt.

Today some finicky callers believe they must use no deodorant, wash new clothing thoroughly before wearing it, and even wear dirty clothing for best results, and not bathe. Some of these methods probably carry things a bit too far. A usual practice is to sop cotton in a mask scent, carry it in a vial, and hang it on a bush near the stand. Or, the caller daubs mask scent on his boots and their soles. This is undoubtedly advantageous. Some callers pin a scent soaked cotton tab to a jacket. Personally, I'd rather rely on my calling ability than to suffer that much.

If you elect to use scents, keep in mind that an odor strange to the region where you are calling may be a hindrance rather than help. It may confuse animals, or make them wary. I must mention here that the well-known Burnham Brothers, famous for their calls and knowledge of calling, once experimented with putting out shelled corn in feeders, down in the brush country of southern Texas near the Mexican border. They wanted to bring deer in, for photos. For two years the deer wouldn't touch the corn. They had never seen any, didn't know what it was.

Many ads offer apple scent as a great deer lure, claiming apples are a fa-
vorite deer food. Not in my state! Certainly deer will eat apples, and commonly do in abandoned New England orchards or elsewhere. But most of
the continent's deer have never seen or smelled an apple and just might be
skittish of the smell. By and large, the consensus is that plain old skunk es-
sence is perhaps the best all-round human scent mask. It not only over-
powers man smell—and if too strong the man himself!—but because
skunks range over much of the United States it is a rather common smell to
most callable animals.

WARINESS CYCLE

A fundamental rule for camouflage and hiding from wildlife parallels
another fundamental rule of nature. To wit, the lower the population ebb
of any species, the wilder and more wary the individuals become. When
rabbits, for example, are in peak cycle, with overwhelming abundance, they
are not especially alert or wary. Undoubtedly this is because each *individual*
rabbit sustains less daily pressure from predators. It is split up. But when
the cycle reverses, the few individuals left live in constant danger and thus
become extremely wary. The parallel for thé caller is that the fewer the individuals of the species he is after, the better he must conceal himself and
the more expertly he must operate his call. The wariness of decreased
animal populations is nature's way of protecting the seed.

In bird calling there is another reason for heightened wariness among
scarce individuals. The longer-lived larger animals—mammals—suffer
sudden die-offs (starvation or disease from close contact) and large per-
centages of the population disappear. But among short-lived birds, while
the above conditions may occur, the usual reason for scarcity is a debacle
during hatching. Adverse weather may wipe out most nests and eggs, or
kill off practically all the young. On certain Texas turkey ranges I have seen
as much as four years pass with hardly any successful hatches. This means
that the remaining sparse bird population is made up of older individuals.
The older they are, the more wary. In years when the hatch of wild geese is
poor on the far-north nesting grounds, hunting way down in the rice
country along the gulf of Mexico is difficult. Old birds have seen decoys
and heard calls—and shotguns—before. But when abundant birds of the
year arrive due to a successful hatch they are often naive, typically "silly
geese."

CLOTHING

Many unique and useful advances have been made over recent years in
camouflage clothing. The first camo cloth, used by armed forces in many
parts of the world, was, as everyone knows, like the kind still used today;
light-and-shadow patterns of drab browns and greens. Jungle-type camo

suits were an outgrowth of Far-East military use. Astute hunters and callers began, however, to realize that so-called "camouflage suits" did not always do the job if worn in a contrasting terrain. A man bundled in a green suit sitting out in waving yellow grass of the plains contrasts too much, and draws attention. Thus some firms began offering sand-colored camo suits, of pale tans and browns. I have one jacket that is reversible — green to sand.

Possibly the most interesting use of camouflage cloth was the introduction of red camo for deer and other big game hunters. All wildlife hobbyists should be aware of the fact that deer and other big-game animals are color blind. Their eyes contain no cones, the cells that transmit color impulses to the brain. Thus, these animals, and also most families of the predators as well, live in a world of grays. Their spectrum is from white to black, with all intermediate shades of gray between. It is very important for a caller of mammals to understand this. Birds, conversely, see colors well, but in varying degrees among the many families.

Colors of course are of differing intensities and contrast with each other. When they are translated to grays, the *color* is eliminated, but not the contrasts, and each shade of gray, plus white, has its own intensity. Thus, and mark this well, color blind creatures just possibly may be *more* alert and observing of contrasts than creatures with well developed color vision. There is less *confusion* in their drab world.

To go back to the red camouflage suits, patterns of which are green or camo, other hunters see the red (for safety reasons), but the prey does not. However, for general wear whenever possible, standard camouflage is probably best because it has the broadest use. A caller, however, who will operate against varied backgrounds will do well to have suits and nets of several hues. The cloth should match as closely as possible the general hues of the terrain. Of all animals and birds that will respond to a call, there are few that do not require the wearing of some variety of camouflage, even if it is only drab outer clothing. The exceptions are a few of the upland birds — quail, pheasant, chukar. However, if you intend to try to call these *to* you, not simply flush them, camouflage is mandatory.

The most successful callers in snow country are those who wear white. We really can't apply this to deer hunters in snow, because most states require, nowadays, the wearing of red or blaze orange — so many square inches — for safety reasons. White applies chiefly to callers after such species as crows, coyotes, and foxes. A good outfit for these endeavors is a suit of dairyman's coveralls. A hood of some sort should be worn, such as a hooded white sweatshirt pulled over the suit, or a white stocking cap works too. Some coyote callers go so far as to use white camouflage stick, as the military uses, on their faces. Wide adhesive tape completely covering gun, stock, and barrel, will not harm it and makes it invisible. Some callers even use white shoe polish on gloves or other leather.

Hunting snow geese in southern rice country, these hunters wear white camo and set out plastic sheets as decoys.

The most unique use of white as camouflage occurs on the southern wintering grounds of snow and blue geese, in Texas, Louisiana and elsewhere. These birds gather in immense flocks and huge decoy sets are placed in feeding fields, as in the rice country. White plastic squares, white trash baskets, diapers, paper plates are all used as decoys. Then the hunters dress in white butcher's smocks to which a hood has been sewn, and lie flat on the ground among the decoys. This is a classic example of ingenious camouflage and hiding.

Archers, and photographers, must get closer to their targets than gun hunters or hobbyists who use binoculars. These groups must pay infinite attention to camouflage. The face and hands *must* be covered in some way, blackened, or camouflaged with the use of a headnet. One of the most successful ruses used by all callers after ground dwelling species is the tree stand. Deer, predators, turkeys seldom look up, and a tree stand, in most weather, gets your scent up off the ground.

When I first came to live in Texas I was amazed to see the so-called "deer blinds." Many are small, comfortable enclosures, literally little one-room buildings, set up on high posts or a wooden framework many feet up in the air. Some have sliding windows on three sides so you can look out but keep wind from blowing your scent through openings in case it might settle to ground distantly. In the Hill Country of south-central Texas tree stands are also very common. A few crosspieces nailed to the trunk make steps to take you up, and a few boards across convenient limbs form a seat. However, if you are going to do any calling from a tree stand, be sure to check whether or not tree stands are legal in your state, and for that purpose.

Tree stands work well because larger animals aren't accustomed to looking up for danger. Here a Mississippi archer employs a portable stand and a Texas rifleman waits in a permanent one built into a live oak.

RULES TO REMEMBER

Most callers, however, will be upon the ground. It is amazing how easily you can err in attempting to hide, even when you think you are following all the rules. Therefore, here are a few cautions. I've already mentioned that a caller should never sit upon a ridge crest. Even if you are well camouflaged, you stand out for great distances. Keep telling yourself to "think wild." If you were an animal, what would *you* notice that might "spook" you. A caller sitting on the ground *beside* a tree is showing every move to wild eyes. One sitting with his back against a large tree trunk masks any movements he may make, and shows no outline.

If you use a camouflage net, a common practice, hang it over bushes, get under or behind it, and tuck in all loose ends. I have seen a flapping foot or two of net spook deer simply because the movement drew their attention and didn't belong. Also, make certain you blend. It is silly to sit against a pale clay bank while dressed in dark-green camo. If you happen to hide standing behind a large tree trunk, *never* peek out around it. You'll be right on a level with incoming animals. In fact, such a stand is bad. You can't see without peeking. But if you must use such a spot, lie down on the ground behind the tree and do your peeking at ground level and through grass or a branch placed there purposely. Watch your shadow when you move with a low sun angle. It may lie long ahead of or beside you. Walking at the edge of cover, the sun may throw your shadow for many feet across the open ground beside you where the motion can be spotted by wary wildlife.

When laying out camo netting, be sure to tuck in loose ends so they don't flap in the breeze and draw attention.

Even though the hunter casting this shadow may himself be screened from his quarry, the long shadow could betray him.

When hunting and calling in a field for waterfowl, lie flat. You'll throw no perceptible shadow and when viewed from above, will lose dimension. In calling situations where light is excessively bright, shadows under a tree will look especially black. Contrast is extreme. I've sat on a stool, using a dove call, not really hiding at all, but just in the deep shadow. Bright, hot sun on yellow grass outside the shade was such an exaggerated contrast that dove eyes could not adjust to both. The reverse obviously applies. The less contrast between light and shadow, the better any creature can see into your hiding places.

Try always to alter the landscape as little as possible when you are attempting concealment. A rule is that the more sparse and stark the habitat, the more noticeable are any minor changes. Once when hunting sandhill cranes in the treeless farm country of eastern New Mexico, two of us made a setup to try calls and decoys in this new-fangled (in our generation) sport. The only blind we could fashion was made by gathering tumbleweeds along a fence row and heaping them in a big pile along the fence near our big homemade crane decoys. Every darned bird—hundreds of them— veered off. That big glob of tumbleweed just did not look right and these are incredibly wary birds.

As I stated early in this chapter, a big book might be written about the intricately varied art of concealment. But I am sure the ground we have covered will show you what you need. You must always keep thinking of new techniques and relating terrain situations, vagaries of weather and wind and the differing personalities of the creatures to the calling methods employed. Learn all you can about the animals themselves. Which senses are dominantly used? Waterfowl depend almost entirely on their eyesight. So do antelope. Predators and antlered animals have senses highly attuned, but their real forte is their fine-honed sense of smell.

CATCH YOUR ERRORS

Also, continually look for errors you may be making. Here are a couple of illustrations, the first rather amusing.

I have a friend who has hunted all over the world. He was so hepped on camouflage that he painted several of his guns, stock, barrel and all, in a camouflage pattern — with shiny, high-gloss paint! Obviously shiny objects — guns, camera, tripods — are instant attention getters, but attention of the wrong variety.

The other incident concerns an antelope hunt I was on with the renowned archer Fred Bear in Wyoming. It illustrates how easy it is, even with every precaution, to do something unwittingly inept. Fred and I, and several other hunters in the party, had built blinds of sagebrush along a stretch of gentle slope above a small creek. The creek was dry except for several pools. In one blind, one of the hunters was watching a pool, within bow range, where antelope came to drink. He had dug a small hole to sit in, and piled sage brush around it.

All went well. Antelope came to water. After jittering a bit, the band put heads down to drink. The archer partially arose in slow motion to draw his bow, and the animals, still with heads down, scattered wildly like quail. This occurred several times. No one knew why until much later. One day, across the side of the pool where the antelope came in, I had casually shot a photo of the archer rising and drawing his bow. When I returned home and had the film developed and printed, I discovered that there was a beautiful reflection of the archer in the placid surface of the pool. Imagine being an antelope, nervous anyway about coming to the waterhole, a lurking place always for danger, and then, as you finally gain confidence and put down your head for a drink, an apparition rises right out of the water at you! Indeed, concealment is a true science, and an art.

This photo reveals why the archer hiding along the bank repeatedly spooked antelope as they were drinking. They simply fled when they saw his reflection as he rose to shoot.

4

Waterfowl

CALLING, especially where ducks and geese are concerned, is so much an integral part of hunting – the chief method, in fact – that it would be all too easy to follow the temptation, almost unwittingly, to write about "how to hunt waterfowl."

We *are* writing about hunting waterfowl here, but only one aspect of it: bringing the birds to gun or camera. We'll be interested primarily in two groups of ducks: those commonly called surface feeders or "puddle ducks," found chiefly in freshwater, and the rafting ducks of larger waters, both fresh and salt, termed the "divers." Also we'll take a close look at the various species of wild geese. We'll cover how to use calls for all waterfowl, some basics about the use of decoys, and things to know about concealment.

Because we have just discussed concealment, it may be a good idea to touch upon that first as a continuation of the foregoing chapter, but with the field narrowed down to waterfowl. How you conceal yourself is dependent, whether for ducks or geese, on the type of hunting you're doing – that is, whether you're hunting from a boat, from shore, in marsh or from an open field or a flooded woods.

CONCEALMENT FACTORS

Both ducks and geese commonly feed in cutover grain fields, or on moist prairies such as those in Canada and along the Louisiana Gulf Coast. Permanent blinds are not of much use in this situation, because the area where birds are feeding may change from week to week or day to day. Also, waterfowl are extremely suspicious of any building or permanent aboveground blind in open pastures. I recall watching geese shy away in flight from a bulldozer that had sat in a large farm field all fall. I suspect they are wary that danger might hide at such an obvious location.

On a marsh edge, this Louisiana hunter first digs a shallow box for himself and implants tall grass for cover. Next he sets out dry-land goose decoys.

Occasionally fence lines can be used as hiding places, if there is grass or brush along them. But most farmers now keep fence rows clean. In irrigated country such as rice fields along the Gulf, ditches are good spots from which to call and get passing shots, but such a hideout requires that the birds be flying in the proper direction. On a strong, cold wind from the north, for example, flocks of geese that are flushed or that start flying will invariably head into the wind and keep moving that way. An east-west ditch or cut makes a good hiding place at such a time. The hunter should lie flat against the south bank and use a call.

In all open situations for either ducks or geese the two mainstays are either digging a pit or lying flat on the ground. A decoy set can be put out on a feeding ground, then the caller lies flat and pulls over him whatever material is a handy part of the landscape — stubble from a harvested crop, such as corn stalks, works well. It is best to find or scrape out a small depression so you do not show much as a "hump" from above.

I shot both ducks and geese one fall in Louisiana from a shallow "shooting box." There were clumps of tall grass on the prairie where we were. The man with whom I was invited to hunt had driven a pickup out on the prairie weeks before and had dug shallow holes about three feet square. The dirt from these went into the pickup to be hauled away. He sank into the foot-deep depression a framework of weathered boards. Then he dug up bunches of the tall grass and transplanted these around the edges of the box. A shooter could hunker down in the box and be well screened from flying birds until they were within range. Decoys were set out surrounding the boxes.

The regular deep pit is standard procedure out in open fields. These require a good bit of work. They are great at proper, carefully chosen spots, but obviously can't be moved. The pit is dug deep enough so that a shooter, even two sometimes, can get into it. I shot Canada geese one fall in Missouri near the Mississippi River in a huge harvested corn field where pits were dug deep enough to stand up in, the sides shored up with planks. Decoys are placed properly around the pit. A cover for the pit is formed of some kind of lattice with small peep holes so that shooters can watch and call but cannot be seen. Along the edges of the cover and atop it debris from the field is scattered so all looks natural. Dirt dug from the hole is hauled away. When birds come into range, shooters hurl back the cover.

IN FLOODED TIMBER

Some of the continent's finest duck hunting is in flooded timber across the Midsouth and South. Here ducks feed on acorns as a mainstay of diet. Sometimes permanent blinds are built in large trees near small timber openings where decoys can be placed. One of these I recall in Mississippi was so large the boat could be hidden in a stall beneath it. We stood in the blind possibly twenty feet above the decoys. The only trouble with such permanent blinds is that the hunter is tied to them.

The more common and often more successful method of timber hunting is simply to wade out into the timber, lean against a tree, and begin calling. Most callers engaged in this method call incessantly, whether or not they see ducks. The point here is that birds may be trading around but hidden behind timber as they fly. Constant calling will pull a passing group down to the spot. The birds are fooled into believing others have located a bonanza. Two or three hunters working together can spell each other. And also, two callers blowing at the same time often rivet the attention of passing birds.

From flooded timber, you can combine mouth-blown calls and boot splashing. By disturbing the water surface, you can create sounds and concentric wave patterns normally made by feeding ducks.

Most of the time no decoys are used. But a unique method of calling is used when birds circle, heeding the mouth-blown call. The hunters slosh their boots in the water, often blowing the "feed call" at the same time. The illusion is much like a big flock of ducks feeding greedily, splashing and sending out surface ripples. The newcomers drop down through the timber, side-slipping and back pedalling, and are in range before they realize they've been fooled.

FROM A BLIND

Shooting at small ponds back in the woods, such as beaver ponds in the north, offers hiding opportunities much the same as southern timber shooting. I've tossed out a few decoys in such a pond, crawled up onto a big old beaver house, and done my calling from there. When hunting marshes too deep to wade and requiring a small boat or canoe, it's a good idea to carry camo net or bundles of cattails or dead grass. Work the boat into reeds, cattails, rushes or other cover and then arrange your net or other cover to break up the boat's outlines. Then hunker on bottom and do your calling.

Shoreside blinds are used on many small lakes, and along rivers. Sandbar shooting is common, for instance, out in large rivers like the Missouri and Mississippi. Use whatever material is at hand for your blind. On a sandbar

Cornstalks make for easy construction of effective blinds.

Located on a small island in a rice field, this duck blind has a roof that hunters can swing back for action.

it may be low willows. On shore it can be grass or brush. On the New England and New York coastal points, sea ducks are hunted from piled-up rock blinds. In other words, it's best, if at all possible, to use blind material right from the area, not something that doesn't fit. Use enough material to hide you well, especially *over* you, but never use any more than absolutely necessary. Spend more time *constructing* your hide properly, and go light on material. Then the blind will look natural, like a part of the terrain.

If you must use a boat for open water where big rafts of diving ducks consort, fresh or salt, then you should put together portable sides and possibly also a cover that can be erected after the decoys are out, and that will also serve to hide you. This can be done with light lath frames and camo netting, or with grass and rushes woven into a framework of wood. The diving ducks react quite differently from the wary puddle ducks and a well-camouflaged boat won't necessarily spook them if the decoy set and the calling are proper.

In many coastal areas where diving ducks as well as some of the surface ducks, such as pintails, gather in fall and winter, scores of permanent blinds dot the saltwater flats. Many of these are wooden enclosures placed on strong stilts high above the water, so the hunters inside have good vision and so tides don't swamp them. These are commonly referred to as stake blinds, and ordinarily hunters are dropped off at them and picked up by guides. Because these stake blinds are permanent installations, birds get used to them as part of the watery landscape.

This crane hunter lies on his back in a trench under a drab net blanket until birds come into range. Then he simply throws back the blanket and shoulders his gun.

Sometimes, when snow is on the ground surrounding water where waterfowl gather, hunters dress in white and use a white sheet fastened to several lightweight stakes as a blind. This can be rolled up to become easily portable, then unfurled. The stakes set into the snow, and the hunter can sit inside. One of the slickest portable blind ideas I've ever seen was a camo job a friend of mine from New Mexico contrived when sandhill crane hunting first became legal. He and others had made some big crane decoys, and learned to use a goose call to make crane talk.

He set out the decoys in a grain field, dug a shallow depression right out among them that he could lie in—on his back. He wore camouflage clothing and a headnet with eye holes and a mouth hole cut in it so that he could blow his call. He also wore camouflage gloves. He had made a blanket from some large-meshed drab material, and he had affixed to its outer long edges some small weights. He stuck wisps of grass or grain stalks into the mesh, lay down in the depression, laid his gun beside him on his left, flopped the blanket over himself and the gun. He could see the entire sky above him, but you could walk right past and never realize he was there. When he got birds coming in with wings set, he quit calling, waited until the range was right. Then, grasping the left side of the blanket with his right hand from underneath, he gave it a flop. The weights carried it clear, and he came instantly to a sitting position with his gun coming up in his left hand.

46

With what was said in Chapter 3 as guidance, and the suggestions here for blinds and hiding, any waterfowler should be able to put his own ideas to work and keep ducks and geese from seeing him. Decoys are a very important part of the waterfowl calling equation. But they are not always used. In numerous instances, if you learn to be an expert caller, you can bring ducks into gun or camera range without decoys, and in some instances in fact you may have to get along without decoys anyway. We'll discuss decoy use briefly at the end of this chapter, but now will consider the call.

RECOGNIZING SOUNDS

Once you're out there in your blind, you'll be hearing waterfowl conversation and trying to imitate some of it. It is important that you know your ducks and geese well, especially the varieties most common and abundant in your area. You should have a good, solid background knowledge of the portions of their vocabularies that are what we might call "safe talk."

Ducks and geese make numerous sounds. Some are used chiefly during the mating and nesting season. These are not of any great importance to the caller, either hunter or nonhunter, because ducks are scattered during these periods and not especially responsive. Waterfowl utter fright sounds, too. Other waterfowl "talk" is made up of the communications used during fall migrations, and on their fall and wintering grounds, in flight and when feeding. These are the sounds important to the caller, because at these times waterfowl are at their most gregarious, and are settled in communicative groups.

Especially among ducks, there are varying degrees of communication. Some species, that is, are extremely vocal, some moderately so, and some quite reserved, or silent. It probably isn't a joke today, what with women's lib and all, but it is a fact that again primarily among ducks, the females are in general the most vociferous and incessantly gabby. Further, and oddly, in most instances their voices are far more raucous, blatant, insistent, loud, and coarse. Much of the time the caller who is most successful is the one imitating hen talk.

Duck callers have learned that it is not very practical, or even necessary. to learn to imitate *all* duck communication. In very general terms, the surface feeders or so-called "puddle ducks" (mostly of freshwater ponds, lakes and rivers) are more talkative than the rafting "divers" of the larger waters, which include coastal saltwater bays and lagoons and surf lines. Furthermore, a few of the more noisy, talkative ducks are also the most wide-ranging.

The mallard is the prime example, with a range over virtually all of the lower forty-eight states, all of northern Mexico, most of Canada and Alaska. Its close relative, the black duck, is one of the prime attractions of all of the eastern United States and Canada. Black duck "talk" is almost wholly comparable to "mallard talk." The puddle ducks are gregarious birds. It is not unusual to find these species in mixed flocks. The several species may not totally intermingle, but mallards, gadwalls, baldpates, pintails, and teal may utilize the same waters, loosely flocking, and the vocal assurances of one species may allay the fear of the others.

Therefore, the call sounds used most by all experienced duck callers are in general *the sounds made by the most vociferous species.* It is as if a duck told you, "If it's good enough for a mallard or a wary black duck, it's good enough for me." Geese are something else and we will get to them in due time. What the average expert duck caller will tell you is this: "If you can

Pintails and coots here share a travel stop. Pintails are good-eating, but coots are not. Hunters often use coot decoys as an "all's well sign" to bring pintails in.

call mallards—among the most raucous and communicative of ducks—you can call any of the surface feeders, and maybe most of the divers." That's close to the truth.

But you should *know* the common feeding and flight sounds of each of the important duck species. This may prove in some cases to be knowledge only for its own sake. It may also give you insight into improving your score on limits or photos on special occasions. On the following pages is a listing of various duck sounds that may be important knowledge for you, the caller, with a section on geese and sea ducks. To avoid confusion, mating calls and fright calls, which are numerous, are purposely not given here.

SURFACE FEEDERS

Mallard. Extremely vocal. Hen: repeated *quack*, very loud, raucous, resonant. Drake: lower pitch, reedy quality, repeated *kwek*. While in groups,
feeding, *tick-a-tick-a-tick-a-tick-tick-tick,* swiftly and often incessantly. The
hen mallard does most of the talking, is very noisy. These are the most
important of all duck sounds for a caller to imitate.

Black Duck. Very similar in all respects to mallard.

Gadwall. Quite vocal. Hen: *quack,* repeated, somewhat quieter and
higher in pitch than the two above. Drake: several calls, deep-throated
whack; a loud *kack-kack-kack;* a high-pitched whistle.

Baldpate or widgeon. Quite vocal. Hen: *kau-awk,* or *qua-awk,* repeated,
also a louder repeated *kaow.* Drake: a series of three very musical sounding notes, *whew, whew, whew,* repeated over and over. This one is a good
general identification note.

Pintail. Hen: very quiet, uttering only an occasional muffled and hoarse
quack. Drake: moderately vocal, calling in flight, *qua, qua,* also a soft and
mellow, low whistle.

Shoveller. Talks very little. Hen: nearly silent, only an occasional weak,
faint *quack.* Drake: guttural *woh,* in series, or *took* likewise, or an occasional feeble *quack.*

Green-Winged Teal. Teal are not very vocal birds. Hen: high-pitched,
repeated *quack,* not loud. Drake: a mellow whistle, also a twittering call,
neither loud.

Blue-Winged Teal. Not talkative, feed silently. Hen: faint *quack* occasionally. Drake: flying: *peep-peep-peep-peep.*

Cinnamon Teal. Nearly silent. Hen: an occasional faint *quack.* Drake: a
low, quiet chatter.

Wood Duck. Very talkative, and also wide vocabulary. When feeding,
both male and female cluck, *squeal* and squeak. Drake, in flight: *hoo-w-eet-
hoo-w-ett hoo-w-ett,* repetitiously in a whistle, with rising inflection on the
ett.

DIVING DUCKS

Redhead. Quite vocal. Hen: a loud *squack;* compared to hen mallard,
much higher in pitch. Drake: repeated deep, cat-like *me-ow,* also a purring sound.

Canvasback. Quite vocal. Hen: *quack,* quite similar to mallard. Drake:
large vocabulary of sounds, a peep, a growl, a harsh *croak.*

Lesser Scaup. Not very vocal except when frightened. Hen: ordinarily
silent. Drake: in flight, a repeated *purr.*

Greater Scaup. Not very vocal. Hen: usually silent. Drake: repeats its
name discordantly and loud, *scaup-scaup-scaup.*

Ring-Necked Duck. Much like the Lesser Scaup or "Bluebill."

Golden-Eye or "Whistler."   Not talkative. Hen: occasional low, harsh *quack*. Drake: *speer-speer*.

Bufflehead.   Nearly silent. Hen: weak *quack*. Drake: a squeak.

SEA DUCKS

White-Winged Scoter   Not talkative, silent except occasionally in flight a bell-like whistle in a series.

Surf Scoter   Usually silent, occasional croak.

American Scoter   Usually silent, a musical *who-oo-hoo*.

GEESE

Common Canada.   Quite vocal. Loud *honk, honk* in flight and on water, also gabbling feeding sound.

Lesser Canada.   Quite vocal. Same as above but pitched much higher, and quite sharp.

White-Fronted, or "Specklebelly."   Very vocal in flight. The sound is of rather high-pitched laughter, *wah-wah-wah-wah*, repeated, swiftly. Like other geese, these gabble while feeding.

Lesser Snow and Blue (Now considered as one species, the blue a color phase).   Very vocal. Several notes: a high, shrill *honk* and a double-syllable, shrill *ka-wonk*, loud, and rising inflection on second syllable. Also a low, deep, subdued *honk* in flight. On feeding ground, gabbling constantly like small dogs yapping.

Brant (American and Black).   Very noisy. *Kr-onk-kr-onk* repeated incessantly in flight, also guttural *g-r-r-r*, repeated.

LEARNING TO CALL

Duck and goose calls come in a great variety. Don't let this fact confuse you. In selecting a call, get a good one, not the cheapest. Some have metal reeds, some plastic reeds. Don't worry about which is best. You may want to try both and make up your own mind which seems best for you. Some duck calls are higher pitched than others. It would be my advice to any beginner to shy from an unusually high sounding call, and ditto for one especially low in pitch or rough sounding. Also, shun calls that won't give you several notes. Some poor calls are capable only of monotone sound, regardless of the amount of breath-force used. Settle on a call that will utter an authentic low *quack* when blown gently, a loud high-pitched *quack* when you push hard, and also other notes in between as breath-force diminishes. Remember that the *quack* is the basis for most of the call series you'll use.

There are several methods of learning how to make the necessary call sounds. For the serious waterfowler, I would suggest he seize every oppor-

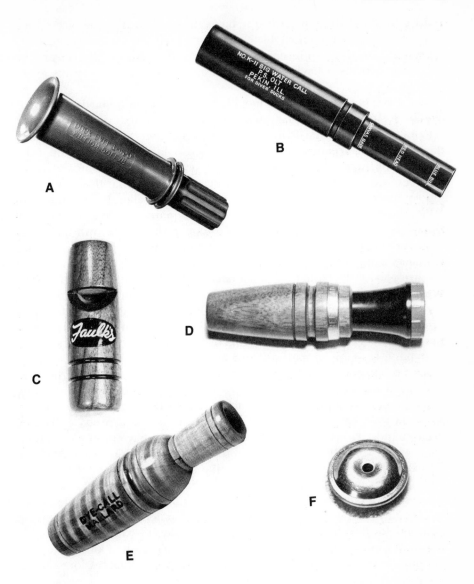

Duck calls. (A) The so-called "Million Dollar" duck call from Thompson Wildlife Calls is made of plastic, said to resist effects of moisture and cold. **(B)** This is P.S. Olt's K-11 Big Water Call for diving ducks. **(C)** Faulk's Game Calls produces this pintail whistle. **(D)** With a tone adjustment to match weather conditions, this horn is by Green Head Company. **(E)** Dye-call fashions this mallard piece. **(F)** Here is a widgeon whistle by Iverson Calls.

tunity to listen to the sounds of the birds themselves. In some places zoos have collections of waterfowl. Listen to them in fall and winter. Spring mating sounds are quite different. Also be sure to weed out the startled or frightened sounds. Check for the pitch and tone of those sounds made when all is well.

Of course nothing serves quite like listening to wild birds. National Wildlife Refuges are well scattered over the United States, and the major share of them are primarily for waterfowl. Visit them. You can get lists and maps from the Bureau of Sport Fisheries and Wildlife in Washington, D.C. On scores of these refuges you can see and hear tens of thousands of ducks and geese during fall and winter, and hear precisely what they say.

If you have opportunity to go out with an expert caller, listen attentively to his "show." Maybe you can get an expert acquaintance to coach you. Of course, the easiest way of all to learn is to do it right in your own home, listening to records. There are a great many excellent records available from call makers. Many of these have been recorded by champion callers. These will give you all the basic calls you'll need,and tell you step by step how to form the sounds. Study such records over and over for pitch and volume so you can exactly copy the calls, and note well the number of syllables in series calls. There are in addition records available of actual waterfowl sounds. I suggest using these, plus records made by expert callers. From there on, it is simply a matter of practice.

Don't economize on calls. For example, the mallard sounds are the ones you'll need most for ducks, not just for mallards, as we've noted, but for general calling of all the puddle ducks. The honker or common Canada goose call is the basic one for geese. With it you can mimic pretty well other goose sounds. However, check out what birds you have in greatest abundance where you'll be hunting. Go in for specialized calls if you need them. For example, there are calls to imitate the loud, shrill squeal of the wood duck, a sporty little duck that is gourmet eating. There are pintail whistles. I once sat in a blind with Jimmy Reel, a one-time champ, in the Texas rice country near Eagle Lake, and watched and listened in amazement as he "whistled down" pintails flying overhead. I shouldn't try here to "quote" his sound. But as I remember, he did it just with his mouth, a kind of whistle that sounded to me like *whew-whew — whew-whew* in quick succession, and repetitive.

There are special calls available for specklebelly (white-fronted) geese, the most delectable of all geese on the table. Obviously there is no point in having these calls if you do not have the species where you operate. But wherever you may need one, add the special call to your equipment. I have been with Lyle Jordan, and with his wife, Pat, both expert goose callers at Katy, Texas, in the rice country near Houston where they offer a waterfowl guide and hunting service, when they each had several calls hung around their necks—one for snows and blues, another for lesser Canadas tuned just right, a third for "specks" with their wild laughter, and a fourth a mallard-tuned call for ducks.

By studying the listing of waterfowl sounds I have given, you can in due time progress from the basics to some specialized calls as the need arises. But for duck hunting what you must do first is learn how to mimic the several important *mallard* sounds, which will bring most of the ducks to you, regardless of where you live. For goose hunting, you must learn how to imitate the sounds of the geese most abundant in your hunting region. Let's start with ducks.

Drake mallards, like these two, are less talkative than hens. A hen's raucous feed call can be heard for great distances and often brings other-kinds of ducks too. Thus, since the mallard is a common duck, its calls are among the most important.

Don't try to make a lot of different sounds right at first. You only need to master three or four. The *quack* comes first. In duck language it has two syllables, the first a bit muted, the last louder — *qu-ACK*. If you practice with a recording, don't worry if your call tone is higher or lower. It is true that there are times when ducks come best to a high or a low call. but ducks like people have individual voices. Make the first syllable of the *qu-ACK* with thumb and first finger holding the call, and the other three fingers down over the end. Open them on the *ACK*. Don't try to make the inflection with your lips. They should stay still. Use stomach and throat muscles and "grunt" into the call.

Based on the fundamental *quack* is a series much used to gain the attention of distant or passing flocks. Some callers term this the "hi-ball call." Start it high and loud, with a pair of *qu-ACKS*. Follow these by a series of half a dozen long-drawn *quacks* in descending scale. The next step is to master what is known as the "return call." This is used to try to bring back flocks that have passed without paying heed. You have to add a new sound for it. It is a brief, quick sound in two syllables grunted into your call that ends with the tongue's assistance in forming the last syllable: *w-HUTT*. Start the return call with a couple of introductory, loud *quacks,* followed by a fast series of *quacks,* at least half a dozen, pleading, the last several drawn out, and then end with the *whutt* sound repeated several times. This is a rather difficult call and undoubtedly the best way to learn it is by studying a good recording over and over.

The only other call you will use to any extent is what is known as the "feeding call." It is difficult to get down pat. It presumably imitates the sound of mallards that are feeding and content. It goes very fast, requires tongue action, making the call say *took-a-took-a-took-a-took-a,* with much repetition.

You use the attention call when you sight a distant flock. If it swings past but doesn't come down, then bring the return call into play. If you think the birds are willing to come in, use the feed call, blowing it not at the ducks but with head down. Many callers also use combinations, "attention" modulated suddenly to "feed" and so on. When ducks—or geese—swing right over you, always keep your head down and don't call. They'll spot your position. But when birds are interested, don't quit calling for good because the sudden lack of sounds may make them suspicious.

There are numerous other calling sounds and combinations that expert callers use. Don't be too hasty about trying them. Become proficient in the basic calls first. A poor caller will drive ducks away. When ducks are wary and you feel you should call very little, you can however utilize the single *quack,* pause, then one more, pause, then a third. This sometimes brings attention to your decoys.

If you study the chart of duck sounds you will note that the divers on the whole are much less vocal than the surface feeding ducks. The more important species of divers such as scaups, redheads and canvasbacks commonly gather in huge rafts or flocks out on large expanses of water—large lakes or the sea coasts. They are exceedingly swift ducks, shorter of wing than the others. They make a half-running, half-flying take off, instead of springing into the air as puddle ducks do. When they land they need and use a "runway," dropping low and finally skidding along the surface.

These differences are important to the caller, because the birds spot the large decoy spread from a great distance over the open water. Once they head at the spread they bore right in, and there isn't much time for calling. However, calling is a help and often necessary to turn flocks or get their at-

The "bluebill," or lesser scaup, is among the most important of the rafting big-water ducks. But it is not very vocal except when frightened. In flight, it emits a repeated *purring* sound.

tention. Note that the canvasback hen quacks much like a mallard, that the redhead hen also makes a fairly similar sound but higher in pitch. Thus with a bit of rejiggering a good puddle duck caller can talk to the divers.

The *scaup* sound is not difficult to make for greater scaup or "broadbills." The lesser scaup, which is more quiet, is not an especially wary bird. Perhaps this is because it travels in large flocks. I've seen scaups come to decoys, take shooting that collected several birds, then turn right around and come back. Buffleheads, usually in small groups, will often act the same way. Unfortunately, redheads and canvasbacks have lately been in precarious supply and there is little hunting allowed for them. Bluebills and puddle ducks are the birds that make up the bulk of the bag.

In order to become an efficient goose caller you must either have opportunity to listen to the birds, or else use recordings. Although geese are wary, in some ways the calling chore is easier. There are not a lot of different calls to learn. Feeding geese are not on the whole nearly as talkative as feeding ducks. Anyway, it is the cries they make in flight that bring them in to decoys. If you are in a flyway where you get only big Canadas, then all you need learn is to imitate the *honk* of this bird. You should split it into two syllables *ka-onk*, or *ha-onk*.

If you will be under snows and blues, you can mimic their shrill yelps with a regular goose call, but you'll do better with one tuned high. You can also imitate the laughter of specks with a high-pitched goose call. But I personally would use a separate call for these birds. The lesser Canada requires a call simply pitched higher than for common Canadas. I must

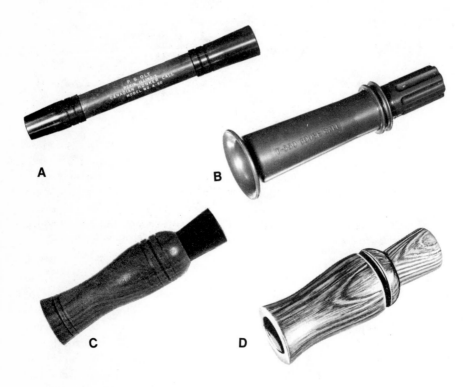

Goose calls. (A) P.S. Olt fashions this A-50 Canadian Honker Call. **(B)** Here is the T-550 Goose Call by Thompson Wildlife Calls. **(C)** The Numara Goose Call is among those available through Herter's by mail order. **(D)** Lohman produces this one.

note here that it is a common supposition among hunters who've had only cursory acquaintance with snows and blues that compared to the Canada these birds are "dumb." Nothing could be farther from the truth. No goose is sharper or more wary than an old snow or blue.

Most beginning goose callers call too much. Geese can be seen distantly. When you spot them, try to get their attention. But be assured that if the flock is huge, the way massed flights of snows and blues often move on their wintering grounds, you're probably wasting your time. The birds you can work best to your spread are the singles, pairs, threes, a half dozen. They're eager for company. The big flocks already have it and usually know exactly where they are going. A flock of Canadas, which consort in smaller groups, can be brought in, however. As geese draw near, you can tell if they seem interested in the decoys. Call a couple of times. If they answer, you reply, and so on. But don't be noisy when their wings are set to glide down. And don't keep up an incessant yelping in a goose spread.

Brant, which migrate along both the East and West coasts, offer specialized and enjoyable hunting. They are noisy birds and easy to call without the aid of a mechanical call. They utter a high-pitched trilling sound in short but repeated bursts. Once you hear it, it is easy to imitate the sound by simply trilling a high note with the action of your tongue. There's little danger of calling too much, or in calling as the birds come close.

A bit needs to be said here also about sandhill cranes. These birds are now hunted in several states. There have been seasons for example in the Dakotas, Oklahoma, Texas, New Mexico. Few hunters are aware of what dynamic game birds these are. Cranes are grain feeders, extremely wary, delicious table fare. They roost standing in shallow lakes, in large gatherings. They are very noisy while roosting. And in flight they call with a resonant chatter. Put your tongue against the base of your upper teeth and trill in imitation of a motor running and you'll get an idea at least of the type of sound.

To date most crane hunting has been pass shooting as they leave or return to roosting waters, and as they fly to feeding grounds and return. Decoys and calls were not available during the first seasons a few years ago. A few hunters, particularly in eastern New Mexico, made huge decoys, and learned to use goose calls in a manner to imitate crane talk. They've been quite successful. Interested callers might try this. To my knowledge at least, crane calls are not marketed, nor are there records. You just have to get out among the birds and listen, then try to imitate their talk.

USING DECOYS

The various "sets" of decoys concocted by waterfowlers is a broad subject that could make a book in itself. We cannot dig deeply here, but a few basics are in order. Because ducks are hunted all the way down their flyways, the birds of today are more difficult to decoy than they were many years ago. Thus, in selecting duck decoys, be certain the colors are correct, that the outlines are also, and that they "sit" correctly on the water. For the puddle ducks no large spread is needed. A dozen to twenty will suffice. But these ducks get a closer look and a slower one than the divers, and the puddle duck decoys should have excellent detail work in the painting.

With his blind matching natural cover well, this hunter has put out decoys for "puddle ducks"—in this case mallards.

Many duck hunters nowadays favor over-sized decoys, some of them two or more times actual duck size. These seem to work well, probably because they are easy for incoming or passing ducks to see. Regardless of size, decoys should be placed where they are easily spotted. If the sun is out, try to place them so the sun shines on them. For the puddle ducks the decoy set should be close to the hunter. These ducks commonly drop down outside the set and then swim on in.

In most areas mallard decoys will help draw any of the other surface feeding species. But if you are shooting a region that has few mallards but numerous pintails, of course use pintail decoys. It's a good idea to use at least some decoys of the species that your call resembles. Ducks land into the wind. Thus decoys must be spaced to account for this. You have to set them so the birds can come in, either over open water or marsh or low ground. Decoys downwind for example, with a hill rising behind, prohibit easy landing for incoming birds.

The only time you can use to advantage a large decoy spread for surface feeding ducks is when you shoot dry land, such as in grain fields. Incoming birds are wary here, without cover. A large spread reassures them. The procedure used by the experts for placing decoys in a field is exactly opposite that used on water. They are set out *behind* the pit or depression where the hunter is concealed, that is, upwind. The birds which habitually land short of a spread are therefore low and right over the callers, eyes riveted on the decoys, before they can decide anything is amiss.

There are dozens of patterns in which hunter-callers have learned to set decoys successfully. Fundamentally they all are based on the same general ideas. Here are a few pointers. If you use two or three tip-up "feeder" decoys, place these near your blind. "Sleeper" decoys give a spread a safe look, but they should be the farthest out. A few coot decoys off to one side, a couple of goose decoys also off to one side, a couple of contented decoys placed on shore when possible – all these touches tell incoming birds safety is here.

Don't toss decoys out haphazardly. Set them in a pattern. They do not have to be all turned the same way, into the wind, as some writers have claimed. Feeding and resting ducks may be facing any direction. But make a setup that, as a general rule to follow, places decoys out from, but on either side of the blind, and leaves an open hole in the middle for a landing field. The decoys can be set in a "U" that has the blind at the bottom, wind coming from behind the caller. Or, if the wind is opposite, pattern the U the other way – the birds coming over the blind from behind and into an open landing. There are setups called "fish-hook" and "pipe" patterns, and innumerable others. These are just what the words describe. The landing field is inside the bend of the hook, or the bend of a down-curved pipe stem. The bowl of the pipe is a group of decoys and the curved stem trails some off in the direction from which the ducks will arrive to land.

This last mentioned pattern is often used in one form or another, and with a large number of decoys, for hunting the diving ducks of open, large waters. The only worthwhile areas for setups on these birds are the prime feeding places, where hundreds of birds may congregate. Most successful hunters watch the birds, then place decoys where the big rafts have been spotted working. This will, almost without fail, be over a dark bottom. Light, sandy bottoms lack food, and the ducks know it and bypass them. The huge decoy layout in this operation *is* the chief "call," and as I've said using a real call on these birds is not as important as with the other kinds.

Like puddle ducks, divers must land into the wind. Unlike puddle ducks, they seldom land short. They come in at sizzling speed right into the spread or else past it. They need room for landing and takeoff, and thus the more open water surrounding your layout, the better. Divers are not anywhere near as skittish of blinds and boats as are surface ducks, but hunter motion will spook them.

Set decoys with substantial spaces between them so your spread looks big and covers a large area. But always pattern it just as for surface ducks except on a grander scale, that is, with a wide-open, large landing field between two large decoy groups. For these ducks especially, I repeat, a string of decoys running from the main spread out into the lake toward where the flocks must come from is very effective. As a last thought, don't worry about the many so-called "standard decoy placement patterns" with their fancy names. The basics are simple, just as I've given them. That's all you need.

Almost all goose shooting over decoys is from land—field and prairie shooting, sandbar shooting in rivers. Goose spreads should be large. It's not possible to have too many decoys. In field shooting most hunters use the same technique as for field-feeding ducks, placing decoys upwind, so the birds glide in over hunters, and when shot at, drift back to flare or climb. Canada goose decoys are used where that bird is predominant, and

A live snow goose sits bewildered among rather unresponsive decoys made from sheet plastic and foam heads.

some goose experts believe these decoys draw other species because the Canada is so wary. That's not quite true.

The fact is, if you have opportunity to observe geese in an area such as the Texas rice country, where lesser Canadas, snow and blues, and specks all congregate by thousands, you will soon realize that the species aren't anxious to intermingle. The snows and the blues predominate, and habitually gather in massive groups. Specks will also gather in rather large groups, but usually by themselves, or else they will be along the fringes of a large group of "light geese." The small Canadas also keep to themselves, or else along the fringes.

However, all of these geese, on winter grounds used by all, will decoy to huge spreads that imitate compact groups of snows. They'll do this because they know that a big group of geese on the ground means both safety and food. Many guides running commercial operations put as many as a thousand to fifteen hundred decoys into a snow spread. Then on the fringes they set out small groups of lesser Canada and specklebelly decoys, to give the "dark geese" confidence.

In some areas, such as the Dakotas, it is fairly common to see spreads where Canada and snow decoys are intermingled. And, these seem to do the job. But once on their established wintering grounds the birds are less gregarious with other species. The big spreads in Texas and Louisiana rice country, as I mentioned in an earlier chapter, are made with white rags draped on stubble, with squares of white and black plastic set on sticks or iron stakes, with the addition sometimes of white foam plastic goose heads stuck atop the same stakes. Halved white trash baskets are used, also rammed on iron stakes. Diapers, paper plates, newspapers—all have been tried. Occasionally big white bird-shaped kites with black wing tips are put up to soar in the wind over a spread.

In snow goose wintering grounds, hunters employ many innovative ruses. These decoys are halved trash baskets.

No pits are dug. The caller and shooters dress in white painter's or butcher's smocks with hoods attached, and lie in the big decoy spread. These unique decoying ideas have proved extremely successful. It's worth noting, however, that here and there hunters in the same region want to shoot only "dark geese." They put out a big spread of full-bodied Canada or speck decoys, and oddly the snows seldom come to those. They seem to want to mingle with their own kind and their color phase, the blue.

IN SUMMARY

To sum up waterfowl calling, the important basics can be simply stated: Conceal yourself well. Never show your face. Don't move a muscle when birds are within sight-range and from there on until they are in gun range. Practice endlessly your calling technique so that it is flawless. Use the proper sounds at the proper time. Use realistic decoys of the best quality. Set decoys to give incoming birds every opportunity to make an easy landing. That's all there is to it—and it's a lot—but the thrills are worth the effort.

5

Turkeys

CALLING TURKEYS is one of the most dramatic endeavors in the entire calling field. The art is also one of the oldest, and was thoroughly researched long, long ago. The early American settlers had brought domestic turkeys with them and probably were surprised to find wild turkeys here.

Southern, southwestern and Mexican Indians had domesticated turkeys hundreds of years before the colonists did. The early Spanish took some of these birds home, from where under domestication they spread across Europe. But communication was poor, and there was misunderstanding about the origin of birds. They were presumed to have been introduced via Turkey and thus were given the name they still carry. That's the official version, repeated in many scholarly tomes. I've always suspected it. But perhaps the name originated as a simple imitation of basic turkey talk: *Turk-turk-turk!*

Over much of the early part of this century and into the 1930s and 1940s, the once unbelievably abundant wild turkey drastically declined. It disappeared entirely from much of its original range in the north and east, and was thought to be on the way to extinction. But management research saved the day, and now wild turkeys thrive in abundance over much of the United States, coast to coast. They are even doing well in those regions where they were transplanted, outside their original range. More than forty states have open seasons, some in fall only, some during spring breeding season, some at both times. And so, every hunter, photographer, or bird enthusiast has ample opportunity either in or close to his own area to successfully call these handsome and regal birds.

CALLING BASICS

Turkey calling is truly something of an art. But old-line purists often make it sound far more difficult than it really is. You do not have to learn to mimic a great many sounds, but you do have to learn to

63

imitate a few expertly. And you must study carefully the inflections and tonal differences and pitch used by hens, young turkeys, "spring gobblers" (that is, birds of the year), and old, adult gobblers. The better you can imitate the bird, the more successful you will be in calling.

However, I want to state at the beginning that a lot of nonsense has been written about exact tone quality. Individual turkeys have individual voices, just like people, or cats and dogs, cows and horses. Hen voices are in general higher pitched than those of gobblers, yet

Up from hiding, this springtime hunter is about to "come down on" a big western Merriam's gobbler that answered a call.

some old hens have horribly raucous, hoarse, grating voices. Very young turkeys, regardless of sex, have high voices. Spring gobblers talk in higher pitch than old ones. But there is no absolute.

I recall sitting one time calling away and getting a reply that was so bad it just had to be an inexpert caller who, like a dummy, thought I was a turkey. The replies kept approaching and I didn't want to get shot at so I finally got up to leave—and spooked a gobbler that had been coming right to me answering all the way. It can happen.

There are a few basics one needs to know about the birds before he attempts to learn calling. First, turkeys are flock birds, gregarious birds. Don't get the idea, however, that you are going to call *flocks* of turkeys. It might happen very occasionally that a whole flock might attend your pleas. But it's highly doubtful. Under certain conditions two turkeys might come in together. Or, you might, without them or you knowing it, have several converging on you. Ordinarily, however, whether in fall or spring, you deal only with a single bird.

Also before starting to call, you need to understand, the loose caste system among turkeys. Under wholly wild conditions, unlike conditions where domestic turkeys are penned or in a yard, the sexes mingle very little except during breeding season. In the summer of course hens have their broods trailing after them, but gobblers stay away and do as they please. In fall the birds of the year have, to a large extent, separated into groups of the same sex. Hens consort together and these are invariably the larger flocks. Unwilling to go it alone, a few spring gobblers (hatched the previous spring) may tag along with mama and some other hens.

Usually, however, these young gobblers get together and form a group that will spend the winter together. These groups are generally smaller than hen gatherings. I've often seen eight to a dozen together. And they shy away from the old gobblers. Small groups of old gobblers hang around together from the spring breeding season on. By fall a dozen big ones may be consorting, or there may be only three or four. Much depends on how abundant turkeys are on a given range, and also the caste system may be influenced by forage conditions. That is, all sexes may be forced to tolerate each other during shortages.

Early in spring the gobbler groups begin to split up. In warm climes breeding may begin in March. In slightly cooler areas April is the time, and in some places breeding continues well into May. At the beginning of mating season, hen groups that are very large split up to some extent. Adult gobblers become autocratic loners. Each old tom has just two things on his mind: finding hens and fighting with other gobblers.

One gobbler will service many hens. He may collect a small harem, strutting and pirouetting, gobbling and "chuffing," wings dropped, tail fanned and chest inflated. As the breeding season wears on, many serviced hens begin nesting and the toms have to hunt harder for partners. When the breeding season wanes, the old gobblers drift off and gather into their compact groups again. Note well that this is a time when gobblers may answer your call, repeatedly, but will not come to it. Right after breeding, if you spot several gobblers together, trying to call them with "love talk" is futile. If you understand these basics of turkey routine around the year, you will determine what you must do, and how and when you must do it, to call a turkey to you.

During spring breeding season, toms put on displays worth your admission price. Their gobbles express worldly desires and serve notice of territorial claim.

Except during breeding season, turkeys live under a caste system that segregates the sexes. Hens, shown here, can be distinguished by their short legs, bluish hairy heads and ashy colored scallops on feather edges.

UNDERSTANDING TURKEY TALK

Much of the time turkeys are vocal creatures. They utter a wide variety of sounds, but only a few of them regularly. Thus, happily, there aren't many you must learn. Some callers try to become expert with all. It's rather easy to fall into errors this way. The beginner should concentrate on just *one*, then enlarge his repertoire from there if he chooses. One sound you must be aware of, and never use unless you purposely want to drive turkeys away — to flush one into the open maybe, or to scatter unseen ones so you can try calling them back together — is the alarm sound. This is a loud "Putt!" It is seldom repeated.

Now let's follow turkey talk around the year. What the birds say at different seasons and the reasons they make these sounds are important. Spring breeding season is the period when the toms gobble. Occasionally on a warm fall day, or if startled, the males may sound off, but gobbling is not common to them except in spring. Toms gobble for several reasons: It is an expression of their maleness and their desire to mate. It warns other gobblers to stay out of that one's breeding area or be prepared to fight. It tells hens where the gobbler is. A sharp sound — a slammed car door, the hoot of an owl — in spring will elicit a gobble from a tom simply because he's "programmed" to talk.

Gobbling begins as a rule on the roost, just at dawn. The old boy tells hens roosting nearby that he's still around. At ten minute intervals he may sound off. As light grows the birds fly to ground. The male gobbles, struts, goes to the hens or starts looking for a hen or harem as the case may be, so he can strut more. Every few minutes he gobbles. If he is with a group of hens and you call, he may gobble but may not come to your hen call. He has all he needs. If he's alone, he's a real setup. By about 9:30 or so gobbling ceases. The turkeys may split up. However, it is not uncommon for a gobbler to begin sounding off again in early afternoon, if he is especially vigorous and virile, or if he has not been very successful in locating hens. Occasionally there is late afternoon gobbling, but seldom in quantity. After or just before the birds fly up to roost, a gobbler may shower down his call once or twice, simply saying all is in order.

During the breeding season, hens also want their locations known. They "yelp," but in a love-sick, pleading manner, with a quavering tone. It is almost questing, with a rising inflection on each note. Visualize it as *Perk-perk-perk* and you can't go far wrong. Or, easier, as *Turk-turk-turk*. The series of three is common, and it requires no more than a second per syllable. Commonly there are five or six syllables. Every few minutes — five, ten — a hen may utter a sound. The gobbler may answer with a raucous gobble, and move toward the hen. Again, he may not say a word and still be moving in. A caller must be aware of this, and stay constantly alert. In addition, bear in mind that if you happen to set up to call and a hen calls from behind you, getting a gobbler answer from in front, keep quiet. Let *her* call him to you!

Occasionally a gobbler may not be in a gobbling mood, and he may also not be actively traveling to hens at the moment. But it is still possible to get his attention. Some callers walk along a ridge, pausing every little while to give a series of "yelps," attempting to locate a tom. A tom silent till now may suddenly give a series of yelps instead of gobbles. If he is a big, mature bird, which is likely, he will probably sound a loud and coarse—*yowk-yowk-yowk*. This is when you should sit right down and continue. Never move from a spot after you've got a gobbler to reply. Otherwise he may go back to the place from which you first called.

Besides their yelps, hens also make a long-drawn whine. They make this call in spring, or may preface a "lost" call with it at any time. They also cluck, and they utter a very quiet, stuttering *c-r-r-r-r,* drawn out. This is a contented sound and also a seductive one to the gobbler in spring. I'd advise forgetting all these at least until you become extremely adept at the basic calls. An attempted *cluck* may come out as a *Putt!* and spoil everything. Hens and young turkeys use another sound to indicate suspicion, alarm, or fright of a level not quite sufficient to put them on the run, but it may lead to that. It sounds like *Quit, Quit, Quit*—each very sharp and quick, but not necessarily loud. Shy away from that one!

When young turkeys begin following their mother, their voices are high and they are always trying to keep in touch with her. *Kee, kee, kee,* they call. Mark well that *this sound and its grown-up variations are the fundamental bases of all turkey calling.* Every baby turkey that strays will call, call, call to beg for a reply from mama or its flock mates, so it can join them again. The mother will reply with a sound that is not pleading but a simple reassuring *perk-perk-perk,* or, as some spell it, *Chalk-chalk-chalk.*

It is important to remember that during any fall, assuming a fair to good hatch and raising success, the preponderance of turkeys on any range will be *young* birds. Some callers are convinced the *Kee-kee-kee* call will bring scattered turkeys, young or old, all throughout the fall. However, the *Chalk-chalk-chalk* version—the adult call—is the call most used. In fall the gobbles, whines and clucks are fewer. They mean nothing anyway now to a caller. The talk he must now use is the "lost turkey" call, for this is the language now most used by the birds. Single birds that are really strayed use it. Flocks that are feeding scattered out use it (with less insistence) to keep track of each other. If members of a flock have been frightened—purposely by the caller perhaps—and have flushed or run off and become widely separated, they will wait fifteen to twenty minutes before beginning their "lost" calls. Then they will move toward each other until all are rejoined. This call is used by both sexes of all ages.

MIMICKING TURKEY CALLS

Now you can begin to understand that there are really only two or three major sounds you really *need* to be able to imitate. And of these only *one* is absolutely necessary; or more properly, you need only two versions of one basic sound. The *gobble,* may occasionally be used to advantage in spring., The "lost" *chalk,* with a softer *perk* version in spring in a hen's pitch, is the important sound. The fall version is full of anxiety; the birds are saying, "I'm lost. Where are the rest of you?" In spring you need a lovelorn version, less harsh—females are saying, "I'm right here waiting, Big Boy." That's it.

Numerous types of turkey calls are available. They fall into two general categories: 1) mouth-blown calls or calls at least manipulated by the lips or mouth, 2) friction-type calls with which a striker of some sort is used to produce the sounds. One offbeat unique kind of call most useful is the "hooter." This call is blown, and imitates the hoot of a big owl. In spring, and occasionally in fall, it will elicit a *gobble* from any tom within hearing. Its purpose is only to fix the position of the bird, on roost or ground. The caller then moves in as close as he dares and continues standard calling in spring, or he tries to scatter (in fall) an out-of-range group of birds so he can try calling singles back. Or, if he hunts with a rifle he uses the hooter to locate his gobbler at either season, usually in spring, and then makes a stalk within gun range, without further calling.

Mouth operated "yelper" calls are generally sucked on, not blown. Old-timers made them from turkey wing bones. Soda straws, hollow grass stems, empty ball-point pens have been used. Commercial type yelpers work well, but are somewhat difficult to handle correctly. Another type is a tiny cannister with a thin latex membrane across part of the top. This uses exhaled breath. All yelpers utilize only "lost" and "mating" cries, and can be used one-handed, leaving the other free to have gun or camera ready.

Some years ago in Alabama a call was invented that is placed inside the roof of the mouth, so neither hand is needed to operate it. It is a small horseshoe shaped item with thin rubber diaphragm stretched across the interior. Homemade models were of lead covered with adhesive tape. They used a piece of a condom for the diaphragm. I hunted with the gentleman, Mr. James Radcliff, Sr., who contrived some of the first ones. He was a fantastic caller. Modern marketed calls like this are more refined. The call is placed in the roof of the mouth, the opening of the *U* facing forward. This call has become very popular. It is tiny and light, hands make no motions so both can grip a gun or camera. The "lost" and "mating" calls are produced with it, and it can produce all other turkey sounds, except the gobble, at any required pitch or volume. The caller uses lips and tongue, and for lost and mating calls silently (voice-wise) makes a repeating *chirp,* letting the diaphragm vibrate. The latex should not touch and be dampened by the roof of the mouth. A good deal of practice is required, but this is an extremely effective turkey call.

Of the numerous friction-type calls, the cedar box and striker is one of the oldest. Today some of these have been revamped in all or part plastic. These are two-piece calls. There is a hollow sounding box with a lip, and a

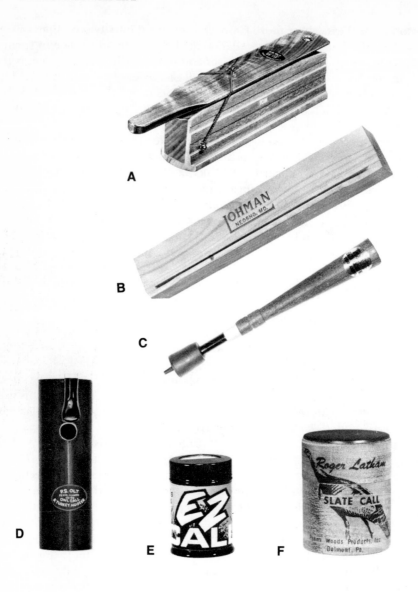

Turkey calls. (A) To operate the gobble box by Olt, you point the near end downward and shake. This causes the lid to slide back and forth, imitating the gobble sound. **(B)** This typical cedar box is operated by first chalking the lip and then dashing a striker across it. **(C)** The Penn's Woods yelper looks somewhat like the old-style yelpers made from turkey wing bones. **(D)** Olt's Owl Call & Turkey Hooter can bring in owls or cause turkeys to sound off, betraying their location. **(E)** Tipping activates a diaphragm inside the EZ Call by Penn's Woods. **(F)** This is Penn's Woods slate-and-striker model.

striker, which is chalked, and scraped across the box lip. Or, the reverse process is used, drawing the box lip across the striker. These calls are compact, and mimic the lost and mating-hen sounds.

Calls in the slate-and-striker category also make lost and hen-mating sounds. These are usually made with a cedar box that has a sounding chamber and is plated on top by a piece of slate. The striker is a rounded wood peg with a handle, roughened and sometimes chalked on the end. The box is held in the palm. The peg is struck against, drawn across or circled around, the slate. With more or less palm pressure, varying tones can be formed. The slate call is very popular, but for beginners it can be a tricky one to operate.

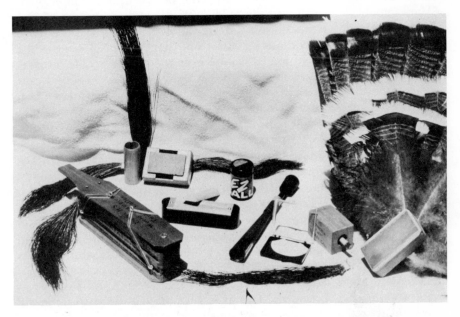

Laid out with various calls are beards and tails from old toms.

The only call that can produce all the turkey sounds, including the *gobble*, is the large box-type call with striker lid hinged at one end. The lid has a handle extending past the other end of the hollow, resonant cedar box. Most of these have one lip of the box cut a bit thicker than the other. One lip gives out gobbler yelps, the other produces hen sounds. The convexly beveled lid is drawn across the chalked edges of the box. Some callers also chalk the bottom of the lid. The lost and mating calls are easily made by cocking the lid slightly and drawing it in a quick series of movements across one or the other lips of the box. The long-drawn *c-r-r-r-r* can also be made with this call.

Under the round fastener hinge at the one end of the lid there is a spring. A criss-cross arrangement of rubber bands holds the lid with gentle pressure atop the box. When you form the various yelps, the bands do not interfere. But if you wish to make the box "gobble," proceed as follows: Take the hinged end of the box in your right hand (if you're right handed), grasping it from beneath. Point the lid handle downward. Shake the box back and forth, sideways. The lid, held gently against the box lips by the rubber bands, moves swiftly back and forth. The *gobble* that results is amazingly realistic. There is only one time for this sound: It is used in spring, to locate a gobbler, after which you can move closer and use the mating yelps. On occasion sounding the gobble and continuing with it after a reply will bring a feisty gobbler to do battle with a supposed interloper.

These "gobble box" calls are a little bit unwieldy to carry at times. Some callers like extra-large models to produce the *gobble* but also carry a more compact call of the same or another style. The diaphragm call and the box make an excellent combination. However, even though the gobble sound is not often needed, in my opinion the box is one of the best all-round calls because it can produce all the sounds. There is one caution. Carried in a pocket, these calls sometimes squawk or screak on their own as you walk. To stop this, place a small pad of soft foam plastic under the lid as you move from place to place.

It is very important that a beginner either have some experienced turkey caller to instruct him or that he buy and study one or more recordings. There are fine recordings available, cut by experts. In addition, I advise listening to real turkeys also. You may not often have a chance to listen to wild turkeys. But domestic turkeys utter all of the sounds of their wild brethren, and you can probably find some nearby. In addition, if you have opportunity to do so, get into the turkey woods before and after seasons when you aren't trying to concentrate on hunting. Take your call along, but don't be in a hurry to use it. Prowl around and listen to the birds. If in spring you hear a gobbler, see if you can get him to answer. In fall, walk across the area and purposely try to flush and scatter a flock. This is the precise procedure used during hunting to get birds scattered so that you can call one back close enough for a shot.

In all states with spring hunting seasons, only gobblers are legal at that time. In some, only adult gobblers may be taken. So be certain you can instantly differentiate between gobbler and hen. Gobblers are taller, longer legged. They appear shiny black because their feathers do not have the ashy markings of the hens. The head of the gobbler, although capable of quick color changes from bright red to blue to ivory white, is shiny bald, and always more colorful than that of the hen. Hens have sparse short hairs on their heads. Gobbler wattles usually show red. The reason it is necessary to be aware of the differences is that many young gobblers have such brief beards they are buried in breast feathers. Also some hens have freaky beards.

With a camo net as screen, this hunter lies in wait for turkeys walking down the fence line.

A Mississippi turkey hunter here winds an old-style yelper that he fashioned from a gobbler's wing bone.

The author demonstrates how to insert a diaphragm call against the roof of the mouth. This call leaves both hands free to operate a gun or camera and eliminates hand motion.

The two-man setup works well. The author, on the right, will lower his head net before he begins calling.

In fall, in some states, either gobbler or hen is legal. You don't have to worry then, unless you are set on gobbler only. Of all the wild turkeys, the so-called spring gobbler—tom-of-the-year—is easiest to bring in, either in spring or fall.

Always keep in mind that when calling turkeys it is easy to call too much, and seldom can you call too little. For example, I remember hunting in Mississippi one year with a friend. He did the calling. On the first series, a gobbler answered. Several minutes later my companion called again. No reply. The gobbler had been quite close. The two of us exchanged glances and the caller shook his head and motioned me to be utterly still. He did not call again. Presently, within a few yards of us, a big tom loomed in the brush. Perhaps he had been suspicious. At any rate, a turkey that hears you and replies knows exactly where you are. Don't pressure it.

HIDING

In closing this chapter, a bit needs to be said about hiding. Turkeys nowadays live in a wide variety of terrains. The Florida subspecies is invariably in dense cover; the eastern variety is generally so, but it now ranges in varying abundance over a great part of its original range—from New York and Michigan, clear to timbered areas near the Gulf. Thus you may find yourself hunting it in a swamp backwater along a southern river, or in timber tracts farther north. The Rio Grande turkey, so abundant in Texas, is found in heavy cover but also commonly in open scrub live-oak pastures. The Merriam's turkey is a western subspecies, a big variety of the mountains, consorting in open pine country as well as in brushy canyons.

Thus, you must match your hiding plans to the terrain where you hunt. I have bagged numerous Texas turkeys by sitting above ground in a tree, calling very little after the first couple of relays because the placement of my sounds would seem wrong. I've sat in camo clothing and headnet in shadow and with my back against a huge pine on a forested slope in Merriam's country. And I have dug right into the middle of a bramble patch in southern Alabama where gobblers, living in dense cover and therefore extremely shy of openings, were so sharp they could, I suspected, count the mosquitos swarming around my headnet and hear the running of the sands of time. Regardless of what variety of turkey you are attempting to call, or the type of cover, be assured that you must be well concealed, and absolutely silent and immobile while a bird draws within range.

6

Upland Birds

The So-called "upland" birds are those usually thought of as birds of the dry woods and fields, the gallinaceous or "chicken-like" birds. Although the wild turkey is rightfully considered in this category, it is so large, and its responses to calling so striking, that we have covered it separately. The quails, grouses, pheasants and partridges are the authentic uplanders. But I have added in this chapter the migratory doves and pigeons, or "Columbiaformes," simply to keep together the game birds of "dry lands" as opposed to lowland or wetland waterfowl.

All of these birds are moderately communicative, although on the whole they are not as vocal and noisy as waterfowl. Upland birds have long been the prime targets of hunters who use pointing or flushing dogs, or else simply "walk up" their game, flushing the birds from cover. In the case of the doves and pigeons, the approach has always been to take a stand on flyways or near watering or feeding places and wait for birds to fly over.

Calling has never been much practiced for the uplanders. Although numerous specialized calls are now marketed for them, and although some hunters or photographers use these calls, no vast amount of calling knowledge has accrued thus far. This is partly because, on a general scale, this kind of calling is rather new, with no long tradition such as exists in the fields of waterfowl and turkey calling. Moreover, there has never been any great impetus for using calls with these birds. The pride and excitement in good dog work on the ground dwellers has fixed hunter attention over hundreds of years.

In addition, it certainly must be admitted that these birds are by no means as consistently responsive to calls as are the ducks, geese, and turkeys. Nonetheless, upland bird calls do have a place. For the hunter they add a unique dimension to upland sport, and at times are also most useful. For the nonhunter the thrills of "talking" with quail or pheasants are in-

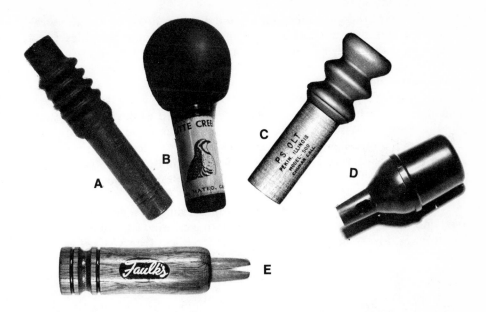

Upland bird calls here include **(A)** a pheasant flusher by Herter's, **(B)** Iverson's chukar call, **(C)** an Olt chukar call, **(D)** a dove call by Green Head, **(E)** Faulk's hawk call, which makes game birds sit tight.

triguing, and for both groups a knowledge of how to use calls in this category should be high on the achievement list. Further, there is undoubtedly much still to be learned in this field, and the anticipation of the possibility of discovery is always present.

BOBWHITE QUAIL

Probably the first small upland bird on which calling attempts were made many years ago was the bobwhite quail. Like all flocking birds that have a specific and rather restricted living territory—birds, that is, that have such closely knit covey instincts that they feel anxiety about being separated— the bobwhite utters a "lost" or "strayed" call to relocate covey mates. Long ago hunters realized this fact and used it in some instances even though they were hunting with pointing dogs.

I remember with nostalgia a week of bobwhite hunting, some years ago, with friends in southern Georgia. An old gentleman, a relative of my annual host, was strictly a countryman. His back-plantation drawl was sometimes difficult for me to understand. He walked with the long, loose stride of the woods-bred old-timer and he doted on his dogs. By the time we'd made the rounds of the fields, the gallberry thickets and the piney-woods edges, we had usually bagged a substantial number of birds and scattered a good many coveys.

By early afternoon the old gentleman, who seemed never as weary as I, would begin periodically whistling the covey assembly call of the scattered quail. Presently he'd get a reply. After several, he'd wink at us and, calling in the dogs, we'd circle around to the general point from which the answer had come. Sometimes we'd find most of a covey, sometimes a single bird. Often as not he'd instruct us to refrain from shooting. He just liked to locate the quail by calling and make certain his dogs could find and pin them down, and take pride in that.

This was one prime form of upland bird calling just for the fun of it. When I was a youngster I used to try imitating crowing cock pheasants, and mourning doves, and occasionally elicited replies. Late years, I've spent many an hour outside hunting season in the brush country of southern Texas talking to scaled, or blue, quail and chuckling over my growing ability to fool them. All such experiences are rewarding, and for the bird watcher, photographer, or hunter they are enjoyable and at least modestly advantageous.

The name of the bobwhite originated of course with the call of the male. It is actually a three-note call, starting with a quiet note, *bob*, followed by the musical and well known whistle, *bob-white*. Thus it should be written *bob-bob-white*, but listeners often miss the first *bob*. This call is uttered chiefly during the mating and nesting season. However, occasionally a male will sit on a fence post or perch in a bush and give the call at other times. This is not a call used to any extent by hunters. A male making the sound may answer a like sound made by a caller, and it is possible occasionally to locate a covey this way. But the opportunity seldom arises in fall.

On almost any bright morning during quail season, bobwhites will call with their assembly call or will at least answer such a call. Coveys will reply best right after they have started out to feed, after the sun is up. Callers can quickly cruise around and locate the general positions of coveys in this manner, then return to find them within each general covey area at any time during the day. Admittedly, most hunters do not bother to do this, but it is a swift and time-saving way to spot coveys, and it is also an excellent procedure for bird watchers and photographers. Bobwhites will sometimes reply during their midday siesta when they have retired to resting cover, and also later during the late afternoon the feeding period.

The call most used for bobwhites is the "lost" call after a covey has been scattered. This is the same as the assembly call but a little more anxious. In various bird books this "lost" call has been spelled phonetically in many different ways—as a three-note *to-le-do*, or as *wurlee-he*, or in variations. Ordinarily, but not infallibly, the call is made in a series of three. Then

In some areas, blue quail (top) and bobwhites are found in the same cover. These are scurrying across a Texas ranch trail.

there is a pause of perhaps several minutes, after which the series is repeated.

Because there are a number of different types of quail calls available, it is advantageous to know the spellings above. But the simplest calls emit a single note. One type is a small, round metal call with a hole in the middle. Instead of blowing it, the caller presses his lips against it and inhales through his lips and the call. This actually makes a single, quite musical, questing call with a rising inflection. It is done actually in one syllable, and might be spelled as a long, drawn-out *wheat*. But the end of it is accentuated a bit as the tone rises in a question. Thus it sounds more like *wheee-eet*, accent on the last. Another type of call is blown but is without a reed. It forms the assembly "whistle."

As I've said, this is not an exact representation. Other calls have such devices as holes on which fingers are placed and then raised, as if playing an abbreviated flute. I have also used one with a sliding plunger that initiates the tonal changes. However, the sound I've described above will do the job. Listen first to how the quail do it. Then try your best to copy them.

This get-together call can be most helpful in locating scattered singles after a covey is flushed. I remember with amusement an incident when Winston Burnham and I were hunting in the dense south-Texas brush country. Both bobs and blues were in the area where we were. Hunting without dogs, we had walked into a covey of bobs and in the resulting blizzard of wings were so startled and handicapped by brush that we failed to get a shot. We waited a bit, then walked some yards apart and both began calling, of course using the assembly call.

Finally we had half a dozen birds replying. We moved carefully for about thirty yards, closer to the general area where the birds had alighted. Then out of curiosity we stood still, calling now and then. We actually brought several of the birds right to us. Although hunters seldom try to do this, it is enjoyable for both hunters and nonhunters. However, because all quail are extremely gregarious, and, when forage is ample, live out their covey lives within an extremely small area calling is used primarily as a location device and not as a means of bringing birds in. Incidentally, if a bird answers your call several times and then ceases, this usually means the bird has become suspicious and "doesn't believe you."

BLUE QUAIL

Scaled, or blue, quail are far more vocal than bobwhites. There are several subspecies ranging over the arid regions of southern and western Texas, bits of western Oklahoma and Kansas, southeastern Colorado, much of New Mexico and portions of southeastern Arizona. They also reach far down into Mexico. These are true desert birds, whether that desert is the cactus country or the high, arid grassy and brushy plains of eastern New Mexico. This is one of the varieties of what might be termed "running" quails of the West and Southwest. Coveys of blues seldom lie to a dog. Scattered singles may lie tightly, or they may not. Regardless, blues would rather run than fly, and believe me they can do a swift job of it, losing themselves so quickly in the thornbrush and cactus that they seem never to have been there. Often a man giving chase cannot push them hard enough to flush them.

Their weakness is that they just cannot keep quiet. They call to each other constantly while feeding and moving. The little roosters crow at almost any time of year. And when a covey is flushed at last and separated, or the birds have been chased on foot and have become separated, it is seldom more than three to five minutes before they begin talking again, and running to find each other. Even though the blue is supremely abundant most years over its fairly wide range, and is one type of quail most responsive to calling, to my knowledge at least no call has ever been designed and marketed expressly for it.

Nonetheless, it is not difficult to learn to form sounds with lips and hand that will call blues because they are quite gullible. Most of the bird books I have read do not give very accurate phonetic spellings of blue quail sounds. Maybe the writers didn't listen, or simply copied their forerunners. Several spell it as *oh-oh,* or *pe-co.* I believe we can do better than that. A two-syllable call is used when the birds are at ease — not frightened — and calling to each other. This call is very commonly used when a covey hears human voices or any disturbance. When blues make this call they are not running, but alerted. Then after they are separated, they use it again. Try to think of a very reedy, resonant call, with rough edges, that sounds much more like *kip-kerrrrr.* The first syllable is very quick and abrupt, heavily accented, the second one drawn out. It is repeated several times.

A Mexican friend of mine down on the south-Texas border taught me to call blues as follows: Place the palm of your right hand flat against your lips, horizontally. Make a loud kissing sound and as you do so, swing your fingers outward so the lips come partly away during the "kiss." Then instantly repeat, pulling the heel of your hand away. The result is a *kiss-kiss* with changing volume and accent. The gentleman who taught me this instructed me to turn my back to the direction from which I heard a quail call.

"The kissing sound is not an exact imitation," he explained, "and if you have your back turned your call is muffled a bit and the bird doesn't hear the imperfections." On many occasions, using this method, I have walked quietly toward an answering quail, calling meanwhile, and have flushed it. I have also watched blues come to such a call.

The Burnham brothers, Winston and Murry, showed me how they use a coyote call for quails. Placing the call just against their lips, they squeeze down tightly and with throat muscles and tongue force air down against the reed, silently "saying" the call. The result sounds like *tip'-tooo, tip'-tooo.* It's tricky to learn, but effective. Another spelling I have seen for blue quail talk that shows it quite well is *check-churrr,* the first syllable short and sharp, the second long and even. There is a very brief pause between the syllables, regardless of the spelling.

No matter how you elect to spell the sound, you can't be in blue quail territory very long without hearing it. And, if you learn one way or another to imitate it, you can induce a covey or a single bird to continue talking back to you so that you can, with stealth, approach very close. Because blues are so difficult for a dog to handle, and often in country so spiny and thorny it is tough on dogs, numerous hunters walk them up. Calling is thus an important additional skill.

There is a quail call originally designed for use on California Valley quail and Gambel's quail that can be used to produce a fair imitation of scaled or blue quail. It is a product of Lohman Manufacturing, Neosho, Missouri. The call tones of the quail for which it was designed are in my opinion higher than those of scaled quail. But by gentle blowing, and forming only the two notes I have given here for blues, it passes pretty well. In some regions—such as southeastern Arizona—you may be in cover where both scaled and Gambel's quail are resident, and this call can be used, with practice, on both.

Blues crow in a most delightful and almost comic manner like diminutive barnyard roosters. The sound is difficult to get on paper. It might be spelled *kew-kow*, repeated three or four times. Or may be thought of as the braying of a jackass on a very miniature scale: *Hee-haw-hee-haw-hee-haw*. The series is done swiftly, quite loud, and with a curious reedy resonance. It is usually uttered when a covey is together, and it is a happy sound. One time Winston Burnham and I, hearing this sound distantly, sneaked up on a bush beneath which a whole covey of blues was gathered. We used the assembly call, getting replies mixed with crowings. We were literally peering over the bushes at the birds before they were aware of us.

CALIFORNIA QUAIL

All quail varieties sound other notes in addition to those noted so far: alarm sounds, mating sounds, and talk of hens to chicks. I remember a long time ago reading an article by a gentleman whose name I missed or failed to jot down. The article told how, prior to season, just for fun, the author used a mouth formed high-pitched "cheeping" call close-range on bobwhites and literally had whole coveys running at him and even individuals flying to perch on the hood of his car. I've never seen this, but I am not going to disbelieve it.

Some quail alarm sounds can be useful, especially with the western running quails, because the sounds help you keep track of swiftly moving birds. Blues call *oom-oom-oom* low and resonantly when alarmed, but they are usually silent when actually fleeing. The California, or Valley, or California Valley quail calls very softly and repetitiously *whit-whit-whit* telling others of the covey to skedaddle.

The California quail is probably the most responsive of all the quails, and can, with patience, be called up practically into your lap. The birds come running to the call, erect, head high, legs flying. Of course hunters seldom —except just for the enjoyment of it—attempt to call the birds in, but simply use a call to locate coveys or singles. The California quail's basic get-together call is in three syllables. I have seen it spelled a dozen different ways. I am convinced the most realistic phonetic spelling is *cha-qui-ta*. This call is uttered in a series of three. The accent is on the second syllable. The call I use is made of two pieces of wood with a slot lengthwise down the center, inside which a rubber strip is secured. The caller's lips are pressed to the slot, the call held by thumb and second finger on either end. The syllables *cha-qui-ta* are formed by breath and lips. Since the syllables are not

All calls here are for bobwhite quail except the call by Lohman with lengthwise split, which is for California and Gambel's quail.

uttered by voice, the result is a buzzing, resonant replica of the California quail's call.

The best way to perfect your technique is to listen to the birds. They're very talkative. They produce variations all based on the above sounds. Sometimes they switch the accent to the last syllable, or lengthen the second one. Sometimes the series is started with the first two syllables repeated a couple of times at lower volume before the take-off into the three entire calls.

GAMBEL'S QUAIL

The Gambel's quail is a fairly close relative of the California quail, and the two are often confused. The chief range of the California quail is throughout the Pacific Coast states, with a few pockets eastward into Idaho, Utah and Nevada. The Gambel's quail, however, is found in southeastern California, in much of Arizona and New Mexico, as well as in southern Utah and in a few pockets in western Colorado.

The Gambel's quail of the Southwest is especially responsive to other native quail calls.

The Gambel's quail is talkative, with habits quite similar to the California bird. As in the other instances, phonetic spellings of its calls differ widely, reference to reference. To my ear, the crowing of the cocks sounds much like *chu-chaaa-chu-chaaa,* and when the birds are running and alarmed they call *quirrt-quirrt.* When contentedly feeding they talk to each other as follows: *quoit-quoit.* These birds respond very well to the same call used for California quail. But an extra syllable is usually added, making it *cha-qui-ta-ta.* The accent is usually, but not always, on the second syllable.

MOUNTAIN QUAIL

The handsome, straight-plumed mountain quail is another westerner that can be called. It is an under-hunted bird, and seldom well known even to bird lovers. It inhabits the brushy draws, foothills and higher mountain burns of the Pacific Coast states plus portions of western Idaho and Nevada. I know of no calls made by manufacturers for this bird. But the single-tone whistle, in a series of anywhere from five to ten, and uttered incessantly, can easily be imitated — if you can whistle — with enough authenticity to elicit replies. You simply have to learn by listening to the birds what their whistling sounds like. Calling only induces replies from them; they do not come to a call as some of the other quail do.

MEARNS' QUAIL

Possibly the most intriguing of United States quail species — because it is so little known — is the Mearns', or harlequin quail. Its range is restricted. Its greatest abundance is in the oak and grass country above the desert floor (to 5000 or 6000 feet) in southeastern Arizona. There are no manufac-

Nearly the whole U.S. population of Mearns' quail is in southeastern Arizona. The male here is the dapper, speckled one.

tured calls that imitate the Mearns' quail. Sometimes it utters a sound much like the buzzing of a bee. It also makes a soft *ch-r-r-r,* drawn out, like the quiet call of a small owl. There is a curious tonal quality to these calls that makes pinpointing the bird or birds very difficult. Mearns' quail will respond, but because they are hunted only in Arizona, and with dogs as a rule, no one has paid much attention to trying to locate them by calling.

PHEASANTS

It is curious that with millions of pheasants bagged annually in this country by hunters with dogs or walking up their birds, few sportsmen – and fewer bird enthusiasts and photographers – have ever utilized calling to bring these birds in. The main reason I suppose is that hunting by accepted methods has long been successful. Calling for pheasants is a chancy sport, seldom productive of large bags, but it is a most intriguing endeavor.

When I was a youngster pheasants were extremely abundant where we lived, and I learned early how gregarious they are. I noted that the cocks crowed at dawn, and again at evening, and that sometimes by making rather crude attempts to imitate them by mouth I could get replies, even during the day. Now pheasant calls are available from several manufacturers. The crowing sound is difficult to get down accurately on paper. It is raucous, loud, something like *cuck-cuck* or *croo-kuk.* It may be repeated several times, swiftly but with diminishing haste, or it may be uttered singly.

The single sharp cry is most useful to would-be callers. It is a kind of assembly call, uttered most commonly during the day. A pheasant caller must prowl most secretively, even distantly, never showing himself to alert birds. At certain times of the year – hunting season for example – when pheas-

This cock pheasant has just vocally replied to the call of the hunter in the back-ground. Sometimes cocks will come to a call.

ants are likely to have been scattered, they respond rather well to a call. In your territory, try to lay out a route to keep you out of sight, and try to find stands en route from which to call, stands well separated. On occasion these will be productive day after day.

When calling this way, be very chary about calling too much. A single cry lets the birds know where you are. If you get a reply, you may wait a bit and call again. But you should observe five-minute intervals between calls. You should stay on a stand, whether you receive a reply or not, for twenty minutes or more. Interestingly enough, pheasants will often respond to this call from long distances, even flying in. But others may also walk in, not uttering a sound. Pheasant calling is an extension of sport in hunting. It requires a high degree of finesse, and offers much satisfaction, though usually with only modest success.

There are two more techniques for calling pheasants that are interesting and occasionally successful. One is a call termed a "pheasant flusher." This call mimics the fright cry of a flushing cock, and has been used by dogless hunters to advantage here and there, and also by hunters at times when the birds were difficult to get into the air. At least one such call is offered by Herter's, Waseca, Minnesota.

The other technique employs a hawk call to keep pheasants – and quail – on the ground and influence them to sit tight. Pheasants are renowned as runners. The hawk call is generally used when dogs give evidence that the birds are running. A piercing *skreeeeee* blown on the hawk call causes the birds to freeze.

PARTRIDGES

There are only two true partridges presently ranging this continent, both of them introductions – the Hungarian or gray partridge, usually called the "Hun," and the chukar partridge. The Hun is not a very vocal bird. These covey birds cackle in a high-pitched tone when flushed, and whistle a single note to reassemble. But no commercial calls have been developed. In the Hun's preferred wide-open plains, where coveys often flush exceedingly wild, it's doubtful that successful calls will be developed.

Quite the opposite is true of the chukar, a noisy, gregarious bird that is constantly talking to its covey mates. Chukars have done so well over past years in the western coastal states and the Rockies states that they have become a most important game bird. They prefer dry cheat-grass ridges, foothill sagebrush, the rocks and brush of canyons.

The chukar does not come to a call. But singles, and coveys, call back and forth among themselves, and so calling is a most useful way to locate the birds. Invariably chukars run uphill when alarmed, or they fly uphill. They also respond best to calling when it is done from below, partly because they don't expect other birds to be above them, after they have moved from a lower place. The sounds they make are several variations of their common name: *chu-chu-chu-kar-chu-kar,* or a long series of a one-syllable *chuck,* or this sound in a three-call series with accent on the first, a slight pause and repeat. It is next to impossible to call too much for these birds. But after a series it is best to pause and listen for replies.

A number of chukar calls are available from various makers. Most of these are made with a wood barrel, to one end of which is affixed a rubber or plastic bellows. This is tapped against the opposite palm, or a gunstock, or even against one's leg, to make the call emit the fast series of sounds.

GROUSE

To the best of my knowledge, no grouse calls are presently marketed, and calling is not practiced for any grouse species, at least by sportsmen. Outside hunting season, anyone can become intrigued in the high country of the west by "hooting" for blue grouse during mating season. Like the gobbling of a tom turkey in spring, the male blue grouse perches and emits a hollow *hoot-hoot-hoot-a-hoot-hoot-hoot*. It may utter various combinations of this series. Indians located blue grouse by listening for these sounds and stalking them. Bird watchers and photographers can do likewise. These are quite gentle, guileless birds.

Years ago I had much excellent shooting for both prairie chickens and sharptailed grouse, and have had some lesser experiences here and there since. These birds are quite vocal and have a fairly broad vocabulary. In fall, coveys of young ruffed grouse often chirp or cheep to each other quietly, but I have never heard of a hunter putting this sound to good use. The only use I ever saw made of their talk was by an old native in Michigan's Upper Peninsula who occasionally was able to flush scattered, tight-sitting prairie grouse by uttering an imitation of their flushing call of alarm—something like *cut-cut-cut-cut-cut*. Alarm calls of *cuck-cuck-cuck*, repeated, are also used sometimes by natives of the far north to flush hiding ptarmigan.

Perhaps someday hunters or bird watchers will learn to talk more effectively with the grouses. At present, however, almost nothing useful is known about their language.

DOVES AND PIGEONS

There are three varieties of doves and pigeons that are legal game in the United States and in parts of Canada. They are the mourning dove, our Number 1 game bird by totals annually bagged; the whitewing dove of southern Texas, New Mexico and Arizona; the bandtailed pigeon of southern British Columbia and the western coastal and mountain states.

Almost everyone is familiar with the cooing of mourning doves. The sound is written in differing ways. The most common series sounds like *cuh-woo'-coo-ca-coooo*. The first accent is on the *woo* which is somewhat higher in pitch; then the remainder of the call drops back in pitch and volume, with the *coo* slightly accented. There are variations. *To-who'-too-to-tooo* might be one variation, and sometimes the first part of the series is repeated. The whitewing has a much "rounder" call, deeper and owl-like *ha-woo-hoooo-hoo-hooo*. But this one also has many variations, from a single *hoooo* to several, or sometimes a quick, deep *took-a-toooo*. The bandtail uses several calls—a big-bodied owl-like *who-who-who-who*, a *hup-ah-hooh* or *hubboh* call, and a long series of deep *coops*. When gathered, bandtails sound much like domestic pigeons and are talkative, especially just after sunrise.

So far as I know, no calls are made for bandtails and whitewings, but several are available for mourning doves. I believe that the value of dove calls

The combination of decoys and the get-together call works well on mourning doves.

in hunting is somewhat questionable, or at the least that calls are by no means crucial. Doves and pigeons do their "cooing" while perched, and are gregarious birds. The whitewing and bandtail stay close to their flocks. While calls do bring replies and certainly are interesting for the bird watcher or photographer, they do not necessarily bring doves and pigeons flying to the caller.

Lone birds seeking company may veer in flight toward a place where they hear a call. But the chief use of dove calls to the sportsman is to allay any wariness or suspicion on the part of passing birds. Calls are used mostly in combination with decoys that are placed prominently in dead snags or bare trees, or even on the ground near watering places or in feeding fields. Most hunters feel little need to bother with dove calls. Curious hunters — and I am one of those — enjoy experimentation. The marketed calls are simple to operate if you follow the instructions that come with them.

I have tried to interest bandtails by attempting to imitate their sounds in the big forests of the West where they range. The birds usually group together, making it difficult to attract a loner.

In eastern Mexico, where the red-billed pigeon, large as a domestic, is abundant, I've listened to their calls, much like those of the bandtail, hunted them, tried to mimic them. Again, they were already gathered and though I could get replies, I drew no birds. By all means try the available dove calls — but just don't expect startling results.

89

7

Crows and Magpies

FOR MANY YEARS throughout the nation crow hunting has been a popular extension of the pest-shooting sport. Sportsmen in the West, in certain areas where magpie populations are high, have hunted for this relative of the crow for years. All members of these bird groups are exceedingly wary and intelligent.

Over recent years there has been a growing trend against sport shooting of any birds or animals not used for food. In fact, some ecologists, with little actual knowledge of wildlife, lately pressured federal authorities into a treaty with Mexico that absurdly placed the crow, and some other pest species, on the protected list.

A hue and cry was raised afterward and our federal authorities then began hedging. The way the law was written there were loopholes. If crows were deemed about to destroy or harm crops or ornamental trees, then they could be killed. The word soon was bandied about that crow hunters probably would not be bothered by the law. Later, federal authorities offered the states a certain number of months of open season on the birds. As this is written some states have an open and a closed season—the latter during the nesting months—and some do not. It is therefore important to check state regulations before doing any crow shooting.

Most crow hunting enthusiasts would have no quarrel with refraining from activity during nesting time and while the young are growing. But crow hunting is clearly justified, especially at certain times and places and in states where the birds are concentrated. In fact, the hunting really needs no justification at all because these birds are excessively destructive in many ways, and hunting at least keeps a check on their populations, although probably a very minor one at that.

Concentrations of crows, such as at this winter roosting sight in Oklahoma, may contain literally millions of birds.

In waterfowl nesting areas, crows commonly destroy tens of thousands of eggs and young. In some areas where crows are abundant, song birds are all but wiped out because of depredations upon their nests and fledglings. In one study where a group of crow nests in a small grove was under observation for some weeks, several thousand egg shells from song birds, plus the remains of their young, were tallied on the ground beneath the trees. The eggs and youngs birds had been fed to the young crows. Along coastal areas where rookeries of egrets, ibis, cormorants and other water birds present concentrated nest colonies, crows often decimate their eggs and young.

At planting time, during harvest and winter, crows migrate and gather in astonishing concentrations, destroying agricultural crops. Some time ago I was sent by *Outdoor Life* magazine to do a story, with color photos, about a crow roost at Fort Cobb, Oklahoma, where it is estimated that as many as *ten million* crows spend the winter! I stayed in a small motel near the roost and was kept awake all night, every night, by the never-ending din. When the birds flew off to feed at dawn the roar of wings was unbelievable. Imagine the nuisance such concentrations can become. They scatter out over twenty to fifty miles or more and gobble up thousands of tons of grain and other food.

I have also seen magpie concentrations in Montana and Colorado where hundreds of birds lived around a slaughter house or cattle pen, or a

91

rancher's yard, stealing chicken eggs right out of the hen house, ruining gardens, even killing lambs by pecking their backs to get at the fat and kidneys.

Thus, to repeat, no special justification is needed for hunting crows and magpies. Further, they are by no means in the slightest danger of declining. However, you don't need to be a hunter to share the excitement of using calls on these birds. They respond well, yet are canny, suspicious creatures, very vocal and always relaying suspicions to their kin. Much pleasure can be had simply by "talking them in," whether or not you are interested in shooting anything other than photos. They can be manipulated in singles and in groups. Visits to some of the larger concentrations of crows on wintering grounds is something anyone interested in wildlife should experience.

CROWS AND RAVENS

There are several species and subspecies of crows—the fish crow, eastern crow, western crow, northwestern crow, southern crow, Florida crow. Although crows differ in body size and in range, crow callers have no need to differentiate calls among them. All have similar habits—which makes calling them easy. Only the terrain may differ for the species, from eastern coastal rivers and beaches where fish crows may gather, to shelter belts on the plains of the Dakotas, to forest fringes of the northwest.

Although the common raven, relative of the crows, is seldom purposely hunted or called, it is easily confused with crows. These birds are somewhat larger, and their deep, harsh croaking sounds are not remotely like the *caw* of the various crow varieties. Ordinarily ravens are by no means as colonial in habits as crows, or as talkative. While deer hunting, I have listened many times to a single raven croaking away back in the timber, but have seldom seen any sizeable gatherings. Further, these birds are commonly birds of the forest and not as abundant in agricultural situations.

An exception is the white-necked raven. This is a large raven of the Southwest. It is commonly and locally called a "crow" and many observers do not recognize the difference. Like the crow, it often gathers in sizeable flocks in winter, around cattle feeder lots, garbage dumps, or any place where food is available. A curious physical attribute of this bird is that the lower portion of each feather on the neck, throat and breast is pure white. But at first glance these are wholly concealed. Many a crow hunter in white-necked raven range has supposed he has collected a rare trophy when he picked up this glossy black bird, and discovered this phenomenon. I have had a bit of calling success with these birds in winter, near Laredo, Texas, imitating their deep squawks and croaks by mouth. To my knowledge no raven calls are made commercially, and the birds receive little attention from hunters or callers.

CROW BASICS

Before you can successfully call crows you must understand their habits and personality. During the spring mating season, crows are scattered and are not in flocks. Individuals are easily called at this time. When the young are grown and leave the nest, family groups often stay together for some time. Young crows, with their higher pitched voices, are extremely foolish and vulnerable, but older birds may warn them.

During the summer small flocks, families and additional strays band together and feed together. Food at this time is plentiful, and thus the birds are not likely to be concentrated for long in any one place. By late summer definite flocks are established.

Crows are extremely gregarious creatures. And they depend on each other and on numbers. Individuals seem to give the impression of arrogance, bravery and general orneriness. But the fact is, as individuals, crows are timid. It is only in groups that they harass other large birds, such as hawks and owls which appear to be implacable enemies.

The number of crows you see flocking together depends to some extent on where you live. Over most of the United States east of the Mississippi, flocks are not as large, even during migration, as they are westward. In the states on either side of the Mississippi, flocks begin to grow larger. The same is true moving from the west coast eastward across the mountains. The overwhelming crow concentrations on this continent are in what may be termed "The Big Funnel," down which the majority migrate. It encompasses the entire region from the Mississippi to the Rockies.

The migration of crows is not determined so much by the coming of cold weather as it is by food supply. As fall approaches the birds begin moving southward. Because of their gregarious nature, their mobility, and the availability of forage, the moving flocks join others, and grow. The majority of the birds will eventually be found wintering in numerous concentrations wherever ample forage is available, throughout the southern plains and into Oklahoma, eastern New Mexico and Texas. Here are the largest winter gatherings of these birds on the continent.

From late summer — when small flocks become established — until the nesting time break-up — after the reverse migration — the groups establish roosts. A roost for a small group may be a single or several large trees. Larger groups require a woodlot. The larger established roosts such as those in Oklahoma and Texas may require several hundred acres of roosting trees. During fall migration and previous to it, roost sites may shift day to day or week to week. Later, in winter, the large roosts are set up in a specific areas. And if the birds are not unduly disturbed, they utilize such roosts sometimes for many weeks or months.

At dawn, or shortly thereafter, crows leave their roost. They do not necessarily all leave at once. I've observed large concentrations flying away for a couple of hours. But generally all fly off in the same direction. They break up into smaller and smaller groups the farther away they travel. They feed, widely scattered, all day. By late afternoon groups start toward the roost again. Usually, as they mass with other groups flying the same route, they will circle and alight in a small woods, calling, arising, settling. This is a rallying point. At last the mass of birds begins to take wing on a set course toward the roost, streaming sometimes in a black skein miles long. On still, sunny days the birds may fly high. On windy days they sometimes skim the tree tops, but not always. On still, overcast or foggy days they fly lowest and are generally easiest to call.

WHERE TO HUNT CROWS

The first basic rule to learn about crow calling, and hunting, is to locate the roost site but to stay away from it. Once crows are harassed at the roost, or too near it, they will move. During seasons when flocks are small, or in feeding areas where the birds have become extremely shy, some hunters cruise along side roads in a vehicle, glassing or watching for flocks. With permission to hunt woodlots en route, the hunters hide their vehicles whenever they spot a small gathering of birds and get into the trees. Then they call. After a flurry of action, the hunters move on to another flock.

Incidentally, when crow calling, you must go the limit in camouflage and hiding. The birds are as sharp and wary as waterfowl, often more so. Earlier chapters on hiding should furnish all the pointers needed. A stand in brush or trees works well, but most expert crow hunters use blinds. These can be fashioned from material in a feeding area, such as brush or cornstalks, or blinds can be portable, camo-net blinds.

The two prime places for setting up to call are the flyway and the feeding area. Feed field setups are effective. But they usually must be changed every day or so as the birds become skittish. The flyway is by all means the best set, and if you do your calling and hunting in a region where one of the huge roosts is located, so much the better.

The plan is to have the roosting area located and to watch the general air paths the birds utilize when going back and forth. Often the bank of a stream makes a good spot for hiding. Cover is usually available even without a blind, or you can build cover that appears natural. Further, many birds are inclined to follow along a stream course. The setup should be made several miles from the roost, if possible. Large roosts offer the best opportunities because of the quantity of birds. But the most action will be had along the *edges* of a flyway, or a half mile from it. Here singles and small groups of stragglers are constantly coming over, allowing shooting without spooking the main flow of birds and causing a shift in the daily pattern. Here you can work on new birds most of the time without alerting the mass.

CALLING CROWS

Crows can be called by mouth, if you practice and learn to imitate them. But this is not easy, and a great many good calls are available. There are also many excellent records from which you can learn the various inflections crows use for specific communication. In addition, this field has been so carefully researched and supplied with mechanical helps that you can use so-called electronic callers. Some of these play records; some use cassettes.

This elaborate crow setup includes ground decoys, a pole with an owl decoy overhead, and a camo screen.

These recordings mimic crows calling to each other, or imitate a great raft of crows in a "riot," or individuals in distress. In conjunction with the call most hunters use a set of decoys. Full-bodied decoys are placed on bare branches in trees. Others hunters sometimes place silhouette decoys, or two-dimensional cut-out decoys, on the ground to simulate crows feeding. Keep in mind that crows are very canny. A large decoy set is preferable. But if you have out only a few, don't play a "riot" record that sounds like many crows. Incoming birds will know something is wrong.

Dead birds can be propped up with coat hangers or forked sticks to serve as effective decoys. Chief crow depredations are to farm crops and eggs of other birds.

If you are hunting, dead crows can also be used as decoys. You can tie them by the feet with stout nylon monofil and toss them up into branches. Or, you can set them on the ground and make them look alive by propping their heads up on small forked sticks or using bent coat hangers for this purpose. If you call crows in snow country, needless to say a small set is effective because the decoys are easily seen. You should dress in white.

Almost all crow hunters feel that the most important item of any setup is a horned-owl decoy. I've seen enthusiasts by the dozen come into territory where a large winter roost has settled, carrying live owls in cages. Then the owls were perched, tethered — and handled with heavy leather gloves — on tree branches. Other hunters used mounted owls. Because hawks and owls are protected species, it would be best to check laws in your area pertaining to these birds. A permit will probably be necessary. However, an owl decoy that looks authentic works about as well. You place the decoy on a high perch, such as an old snag or a pole brought for the purpose, so the crows spot it easily.

The reason the owl is so effective is that it is a natural enemy of crows and seems to greatly excite them. No individual crow is brave enough to take the owl on, but a big gang will circle and dive, all of them screaming hatred. It is a good plan to use a recording of crows rioting over an owl, keeping the volume up to alert distant birds. But as they come close the volume should be lowered. Also, if you become adept at blowing a call, you can usually handle the situation better by letting the crow gang make the big racket after they've arrived. Turn off the player, and use your mouth call. Two or three hunters all calling adds to the racket. The speaker of any player, incidentally, should be out away from the blind and concealed. If it is beside you, you call attention to your hide. Incidentally, at times you can drive crows wild by blowing a hawk call, or making a growling hoot with a turkey "hooter" to imitate owl cries, while the riot record is playing, or else mixing it in with your own calling.

CROW LANGUAGE

Some callers attempt to divide the language of crows into numerous sounds with different meanings. While it is possible that these people may be right, beginners find the wide range of "talk" confusing. Even for old hands too varied a "talk" arsenal leads to errors that can drive the birds away. The basic call which everyone must learn is the series, usually in threes, of brief, sharp caws—*caw-caw-caw*. These are abrupt, and loud, and are used by crows trying to locate or keep in touch with other crows as they move along a flyway, perhaps strung out over long distances and over a wide flight lane.

But this query call is also used to locate birds that have found a good foraging spot. It may be that this is the main purpose of it. Since the caller operates from ground level, he should, at medium to close range, reply with what can be termed the "feed" call. This is a slower-spaced series, also generally in threes, in which each syllable is not chopped off, but is drawn out—*caaaawww*. Because flying crows talk to each other while in flight with the short, abrupt notes, two callers—or even a single—commonly intermix the query and feed sounds, turning away to slightly muffle one, back for the other.

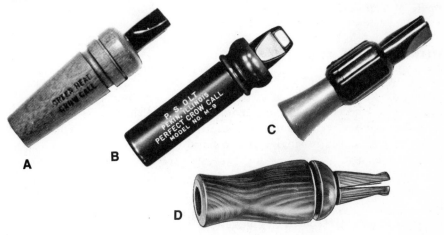

Crow calls. (A) This Green Head horn consists of walnut and plastic. **(B)** Hard rubber, here is Olt's model. **(C)** With rotating sleeve, this Green Head instrument can be tuned to sound like an old or a young crow. **(D)** Lohman's piece also imitates most of the crow sounds.

As I've stated, it is best by far to use decoys. If you utilize only crow decoys, your object in calling is to get flying birds to hear and look your way, and thus spot the decoys. You then hope they'll come to have a look, as you cajole them. Of course, an owl decoy presents another situation. The recorded riot call will usually do the best job of bringing birds in. But a caller can mimic the fight sound the birds make, too. Be sure to listen to it on a how-to-call record or from the birds themselves. The fight sound is difficult to write phonetically, but it is deep and extremely hoarse and raucous, like a grating, loud *grrrrrr,* repeated over and over. Growl into your call as you blow and you'll have a fair representation.

Remember, when trying this fight or riot call, that the birds also will be trying to rally support. So, many of them as they gather will continue imploring others to come in, to answer. To do this they use the "query" call, very sharp and loud, intermingled with the fight. Two or more callers producing such a combination often work birds up to lose all caution. I have watched hiding hunters toss dead crows into the air, and pitch one or more onto the ground below the owl decoys. This occasionally drives the gathered, circling birds wild.

These are really all the crow sounds you need. However, distress sounds are used on cassettes, and other anguished sounds simulating a crow mournfully pleading, as if injured. Admittedly, these are extremely effective. So are the cries of young crows, especially in distress. But those should be used only in summer. Recordings help teach you to make these, or you can play them on your recorder instead of attempting to imitate them with a blown call. Some calls are adjustable, to make high-pitched cries of young birds, as well as normal sounds of adults.

HOW TO CALL MAGPIES

I have included magpies in this chapter because I personally think they are among the most intriguing of birds for a caller. The old saying that refers to someone who "chatters like a magpie" well describes these noisy, talkative birds. They are gregarious, gathering in groups but also spending much time scattered in singles or two's and three's. Where food is abundant, such as near a slaughter house or cattle feeder lot, there may be several hundred. However, magpies are not present in as great an abundance as crows, and are not migratory, or they might form larger wintering numbers.

The common black-billed magpie ranges from the western Great Plains to the eastern slope of the coastal mountains along the Pacific, and from Alaska to Arizona and occasionally western Texas. There is one other variety, the yellow-billed magpie, found in portions of the interior California valleys. Magpies are extremely handsome birds, dapper in black and white with their streaming tails and lilting flight. Their personality hardly

Here a magpie has come to a wildly blown coyote call and flares suddenly as he realizes his mistake.

matches. And though certainly no pest shooter wants to eliminate magpies from the west, a good many persons in their range, wherever they gather in concentrations, are always glad to have some of them eliminated.

There is little danger that hunters could bring the magpie population low. Magpies are without question the sharpest, most crafty birds awing. That's what makes them sport to call, even if you do it just for photos or for fun, without any shooting. The magpie is a real challenge. I've hidden in a hay stack where these "scads" had been consorting, and not a one came near again until I'd left. Yet they are brazen around ranch and farm yards and fields, seeming to sense whether or not a potentially dangerous human is about.

Magpies ruin a great many game bird nests, eating the eggs and young of prairie grouse and pheasants. They pursue fresh branded calves, snatching hunks of flesh from the raw brand. I was staying on a Colorado ranch one time where magpies found small holes to squeeze through into the chicken house and whack open eggs before the rancher's wife got to them. They also had chased and pecked her cat until it was bloody.

The most interesting magpie story I've come across was told to me by a western rancher who did some winter fur trapping. He marked his stream bottom traps by thrusting a stick into the ground with a bit of fluttering white cloth tied at the top. This made trap locations quick to find. Magpies were curious about the cloth. Investigating, they discovered trapped animals, and ate holes in them, dead or alive.

There are no commercial magpie calls. I got onto the idea of calling them on several different western jaunts during which I was using a coyote call. I discovered that scattered birds seemed to be very much interested in the anguished "dying rabbit" cry. Since magpies will eat almost anything, as I've already indicated, here and there a bird or two would come right to the call. Then during antelope and mule deer hunts, I began watching the entrails after we'd taken the animal in. One time I hid in tall sage near antelope entrails and started blowing the coyote call. Soon several birds flew across. When they noticed the offal, I continued calling but very low. They circled right over within a few feet of the sage bushes.

Baiting and calling works quite well. Any kind of garbage or carrion will do. But if you intend to shoot anything more than pictures, you'll have to keep moving the bait to other spots. Once shot at, magpies simply will not return.

They have roost sites quite similar to those of crows, except that they will utilize low brush, such as willows, on the plains and in foothills. You can get shooting, and pictures one time only at a roost site, and never again. The birds will move. However, by locating a roost, watching the morning and late afternoon flight patterns, you can establish general flyways.

Now the technique is to set up perhaps a half mile to a mile away, where forage may be abundant, or if not there, where cover is available, such as in low brush. Two callers working together can do better than one. And this two-caller method works marvelously. The Burnham brothers and I just stumbled upon it a few years ago while putting in a lazy afternoon during a deer hunt in Colorado.

The object is to sneak into low willows without any birds spying you. If one does, it will most certainly alert others. Finally, when well concealed, one caller begins blowing a coyote call. Not properly, but with wild screaming and wailing. The other, sitting a few yards away, now begins caterwauling exactly the same. Both keep it up together. For some reason this crazy sound arouses an insatiable curiosity in the birds. On the first try, we were only fiddling around to see how they would react. We were astonished when several came swooping over us, screeching away to add to our din.

These birds circled, and brought more. During that first experiment we had possibly a hundred circling round and round. Oddly, even though we shot a few, as long as the screaming continued the birds keep circling and swooping. Later I learned to pick up dead birds and throw them up high above the willows as I saw birds approaching. Sometimes certain individuals acted as though they intended to intercept the dead bird in the air.

In Montana I tried this same calling, and two of us kept flinging camouflage caps into the air, from one hiding place. Curiosity again. The birds could not figure this out, and kept wheeling over. After a bit, of course, they tire of it, become bored or suspicious, and leave. Again, this is not a sport in which you down scores of birds. But it is intriguing, and a good way to observe these interesting birds and get photos. Trying to approach magpies, with even 300 mm. telephoto lens, close enough to get a respectable image on film is all but impossible. I suspect much more might be learned about fooling magpies. And of course the best way to increase calling effectiveness is to experiment.

A handsome bird, the magpie is also an exasperating pest that steals eggs, damages gardens and kills lambs by pecking their backs to get at the kidneys.

8

Deer

It Is Paradoxical that deer, the most abundant and most hunted American big game animals, are rarely called by sportsmen and wildlife observers. Part of the lack of attention to calling deer is that other traditional methods have for so long been consistently successful that only a scattering of hunters ever considers calling deer. Chiefly, however, it is not so much lack of interest as the fact that most people interested in deer either don't realize calling can be successful, or else don't believe it.

As I stated in an earlier chapter, deer are silent most of the time. Many hunters have spent a lifetime of deer seasons without ever hearing a deer make a vocal sound. The most common noise made by deer is the snort, used more by whitetails than by mule deer, a sound indicating suspicion, and finally fright. This sound, the hunter produces by mouth, is sometimes used to flush hiding deer from canyons or brush. Also, as I mentioned earlier, whitetails can be flushed from brush by a hunter loudly blowing a predator call.

There are two methods of bringing deer to the caller. One is by blowing a deer call. This may get results at any time of year. Unquestionably much experimentation needs to be done in this field, by numerous hunters, photographers or wildlife hobbyists, for there is a lot still to be learned about it. Sometimes it works perfectly, sometimes poorly. The other calling method is rattling antlers to bring in bucks. This is effective only during the rut, and it is one of the most dramatic of all calling endeavors.

USING SCENTS

We touched earlier on the use of scents. I have always felt that advertising scents as useful for "calling" deer is stretching the point just a bit. In deer

102

the puzzling aspects about using a call for deer. It can be totally ineffective, or startlingly effective. It's hard to achieve consistent results of a routine sort, but this, no doubt, is because so few callers have worked with the idea long enough. Without question the lack of success stems from ineptitude on the part of the caller.

Even some marketed deer calls are improperly conceived. The call is quite similar to a predator call but it should be pitched much lower. The bleat or *Baaaaa* is formed by holding and blowing the call much like a duck call. The last three fingers close around the end at the beginning, and open up. In another case, the left palm is cupped over the end and as the call is blown this muting is partially opened. The latter is particularly effective when attempting to imitate an anguished bleat or cry. For the ordinary bleat, blow gently. Keep in mind that the fawn or young deer voice, though it carries well, is not loud, and, it quavers. You can make the sounds by using a predator call that is pitched a bit low, or with one that supposedly imitates the cry of an injured jack rabbit, which is much lower and more raucous than the cottontail voice. It is best however, to use a call made and tuned for deer.

The great fault of most deer callers is that they call too much. Think how seldom — if ever — you've heard a fawn bleat. Give a couple or three quavering bleats, then keep quiet for ten or fifteen minutes. Further, don't expect an answer. You might get one, but it's not likely. Keep watch for deer circling to get the wind on your position. Still days are, of course, best for calling and hunting. Some deer may come very slowly. If you see one hunting your spot, don't be tempted into calling again. Let well enough alone. Does and young bucks are usually the most interested. But as I've indicated, now and then a mature buck simply rushes the sound.

I have read instructions about calling while whacking a stick on the ground to imitate the sound of a deer pounding its forefoot. I've never had any heightened results from this practice. It may indeed arouse further curiosity. It may also disturb deer, because suspicious or uncertain deer often do it themselves. A deer call is a handy implement to carry even if you don't try to bring deer to you. Learn to operate it properly, and when you see a deer with its head behind brush, or down, feeding, and you want to look it over, blow the call. Almost without fail the deer will raise its head, curious, listening. Walking or running deer — not spooked by the hunter — can sometimes be stopped by blowing a call. They may not come to you but will listen and look.

One of the reasons I have emphasized that much can still be learned about deer calling, is that here and there I — and others — have had experiences that are contrary to what I have just written. In the West I've seen mule deer — big bucks — just come barreling through the timber or across the foothills to the sound of a coyote call, the caller really pouring it on. It is possible they interpret the call as the sound of an anguished deer. Mule deer, remember, are exceedingly gregarious and interested in their companions. I have seen a buck shot from a group—in one instance a group of seven that I'd observed hanging together for some days—and as the buck dropped, the others scattered momentarily, then came back to surround and look at their fallen companion—an unsettling scene.

At any rate, mule deer sometimes are drawn to loud calling, whether with deer or coyote calls. The Burnham brothers were early experimenters with deer calls. On Vermejo Park Ranch in northern New Mexico the Burnhams had mule deer practically running over them some days. They tried calling in a way exactly opposite to the one I have described—blowing in anguished bellows and bleats and cries of distress as loud and wildly as they could. This seemed to excite the deer tremendously. But remember, these were mule deer, and in an undisturbed area. The same process will put every whitetail out of the country.

To sum up mouth-blown calls, my own opinion is that mule deer respond better to them than whitetails; that a whitetail hunter who will settle for a doe has a fair chance at success when using a call; that a non-hunting caller can at least have much pleasure and some dramatic moments by calling deer anywhere, at any time of year. For whitetails I believe the quiet, authentic fawn-bleat call works best. For mule deer, this call gets response at times, and so does the loud, wild distress call. Again I wish to emphasize, broad use of calls and experimentation with them is what is needed for better understanding, and response. Some years ago I corresponded with a man in Pennsylvania who claimed to have kept meticulous records and to have called, year-round over the years, over 900 whitetails! Once when I did a magazine piece about deer calling I had letters from all over the nation relating successful incidents. So, calling works—sometimes. Even "sometimes" is highly intriguing and dramatic.

RATTLING ANTLERS

This brings us to the rut and to rattling antlers. Does very seldom come to this sound. Bucks respond in various ways. Some will come on the run, hackles raised, eyes wild. Some come sneaking silently. Some approach very slowly. Bucks come to the sound because it represents the sound of two other bucks fighting. Some of them unquestionably come ready to fight. During the rut there is of course competition for does, but each buck has his own bailiwick staked out and he doesn't intend to tolerate other bucks on his home grounds. However, many a buck that comes pussyfooting to your stand has ideas other than fighting in mind: He intends to run off with the "doe" the other bucks are fighting over.

Whitetails respond to rattled antlers better than mule deer, and it was the positive response that led to the development of this calling technique. But both types of deer *will* respond to rattled antlers. Young, spike bucks often put on a preposterous and comic show when they come to rattled antlers. I've had one approach so close I could touch it; then it looked at me in disbelief and ran off a few steps, but when I quietly rattled again it whirled and came right back. If you are rattling and a young buck comes in, always watch it carefully. If it keeps looking back over its shoulder, or at some other spot, and seems uneasy, it's almost a sure sign that a big buck is moving in. The spike doesn't want to get in a fight he can't handle, yet he is overwhelmingly intrigued by what's happening.

Not all deer hunting seasons fall during the rut. But a hunter or wildlife hobbyist can have much enjoyment regardless, just "rattling bucks" for fun. The more dense the deer population, the more likely you are to get good results. Also, during a season when the rut happens to be very concentrated, with all the bucks "running" at one time for a period of a couple of weeks, success is always better, because competition for does is more severe.

No one is quite certain where the art of rattling antlers originated. But the area where it has been in use for many years and from which deer hunters first heard of it is the so-called "brush country" of southern Texas. This is an area of dense thornbrush and cactus. It has an excellent population of large whitetail deer. This is difficult hunting country, and it's often hard to see deer there. Long ago Mexicans and old-time Texas deer hunters used rattling to get bucks out of the brush for shooting.

I can recall that as recently as fifteen years ago many hunters claimed that rattling antlers would work successfully *only* in the Texas Brush Country. Then people began trying it a couple hundred miles north of the border, in the so-called "Hill Country" where I presently live and where there is an extremely dense whitetail population. Calling was just as successful here as farther south in the brush. When I did a story about this phenomenon for one of the national magazines, urging hunters everywhere to try it, I began getting letters from various parts of the country from interested sportsmen. I continued correspondence with some of these, and had soon substantiated the fact that whitetails had been rattled up in a number of other states — North Dakota, Minnesota, New Hampshire, and Pennsylvania among them.

The fact is of course that rattling will bring in bucks anywhere, if done at the proper season, and in an area where there is a good chance that deer will hear the sound. The rumor still persists that "it won't work" anywhere but in southern Texas. That's simply untrue.

To get started rattling you have to understand buck habits during the rut. Scout your area and look first of all for buck "rubs." These are made by bucks polishing their antlers and engaging in mock battles with bushes or saplings. Small branches will be broken, and the bark invariably scraped from the sapling trunk. If you can locate several rubs in an area of modest

With the approach of rut, bucks begin sparring with trees and branches, causing rubs like this one.

size, you can be sure that one or more bucks live here. This will be a good spot to try rattling.

However, a more important sign is a "scrape." The scrape is made by a buck in rut. It is a pawed-up spot on the ground and will seldom be in a dense thicket. Almost without fail it will be on an "edge" somewhere, in soft, dry earth. Right above, overhanging, there will be a branch, usually a leafy one. This will be at a height the deer can reach with its antler tips, and its nose. The buck urinates in the scrape, and usually also on his hocks. The scent glands on the hind leg are flared and wet with exuded musk at this time also. While at the scrape, the buck will reach up and gently rake his antler tips against the overhanging branch, and then reach up and nuzzle it with mouth and nose. Just why this routine is performed is anybody's guess. But the urine in the scrape and the musky scent left by the deer is his "sign" to does in the area that he is "at home" and in breeding form.

The scrape also marks a boundary of this buck's domain. He may make other scrapes in his territory. He does not want, and usually won't tolerate, raids by other bucks into his area and the scrapes are a warning, or a challenge, to interlopers. Does ready to be bred will commonly follow a buck's scent trail and they, too, will urinate in his scrapes. This is their message. A scrape that is obviously in use is a positive sign that a buck in rut will make the rounds and come here again and again. Thus, taking a stand for rattling near a scrape is just certain to bring a buck, for the sound, to him, indicates that other bucks are raiding his staked-out "running grounds."

Of course, you don't need to set up at such spots. Much depends on hiding opportunities near by. But if you locate one or more scrapes, your chances of rattling up a buck in the area are excellent. Sometimes the results of rattling at a good stand are amazing. A few years ago while producing a film about antler rattling, I had four bucks come running in from various directions to the same spot.

Obtaining a proper pair of rattling antlers is important. They should be uniform, and at least four points on a side, including the brow tine. I like these antlers—from an eight-point (full count) deer—better than those with more points. Fairly long tines are important, and the set should be a good size, but not unwieldy. If you are a deer hunter, you may have a proper set somewhere. If not, you'll just have to "collect" them on a hunt, or ask help of a few hunter friends. The only place I ever knew that sold rattling antlers was the Burnham Brothers, Marble Falls, Texas 78654.

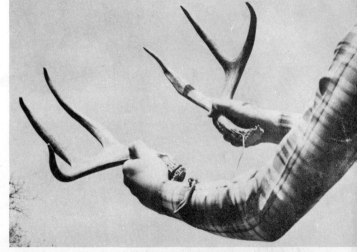

This set has sufficiently long tines yet is not unwieldy. To begin, hold the antlers about the way a buck would wear them. Start with a sharp, loud clap and follow by meshing and rattling the tines. Then repeat, trying to envision two bucks hooking and pushing. For added effect, rake the ground with one antler while whacking and raking the bushes and tree bark with the other. Once you have a buck in view, you may be able to bring him in closer by gently and artfully tickling the tines.

Here the author glasses a clearing with a good set of rattling antlers over his shoulder. He has sawed the brow tines off these.

To prepare the set, saw the individual antlers from the skull. Some old hands at rattling saw them off just above the burl. I cut just below, to leave the burl on. The brow tines should now be smoothly sawed off. Any small knobs or points should also be cut off so they won't hurt your hands. Some hunters also cut the sharp antler tips off. Following the cutting, all sawed surfaces should be filed down smooth. If you have cut above the burl, then drill a small hole through the base of each antler, so you can tie a leather thong between, for carrying the set over your shoulder and for keeping the antlers together. I file the burl some to smooth it, and tie the thong just above it.

The antlers are held for rattling just the way the deer wore them, left in your left hand, right in right. Gripped firmly by the bases, they can now be brought together so they mesh properly. When you carry them out hunting, either hang them over a shoulder or else stack them and grip both in one hand. You don't want any inadvertent rattling as you walk to your stand.

In selecting a stand, don't pick a place overlooking a broad, coverless valley. Whitetails will not cross large open places. A small woods opening is

110

best. Be sure you have a good place to hide, and wear camouflage. Sit so you can watch all around the opening. Usually bucks will come along the edges, not directly across. If there are scattered bushes, you can bet a buck will slip around each, using them as cover even though moving swiftly. A very still, frosty dawn is the best time for rattling. If there is a stiff wind chances are poor. If there is a mild breeze, sit facing downwind, but situated so that you can watch both sides—an entire 180 degree arc. Any deer coming to the sound will circle to get the wind on your spot. Once it does so, it will probably leave. At such times mask scents are a good idea. That and a musk scent, may be of some help. Invariably, however, it is on the still dawns that results are best.

Get out at your spot right at dawn. Rattle for fifteen or twenty mintues. Usually if you get no results by then you might as well move. I try to have a series of places staked out ahead of time. The move should be long enough to get you well outside the first area. A half mile or more is best. From dawn until about 9:30 is a "hot" period. By 9:30 the deer will be bedding down. I once got a buck out of its bed and brought it in by staying with it for a full hour—the deer distantly in sight and cautiously moving in all the time. But usually results are uncertain after mid-morning. You may bring bucks in late in the afternoon when they begin to move again.

If you are operating alone, be sure to have gun or camera ready and in quick reach, for you may be startled to have a big buck come running right at you. The best way to work is with two people, one with camera or gun, the other doing the rattling. The procedure is quite simple, but it pays to select the stand with care. Get a good sitting spot where, if possible, there is some gravel or small rocks, a leafy bush, and a tree with rough bark, all within reach.

Though both whitetail and mule deer bucks can be rattled up, whitetails respond better. Their styles of approach may range from blustery to stealthy.

Here's the routine I usually employ. I give the antlers a sharp, loud clap together, immediately follow it by meshing them and rattling the tines. Then another clash or two and more rattle. Try to visualize two bucks with heads together, twisting and turning. I then rake gravel or stones with the points of one antler, whack and rake the bush with one, and scrape the tree bark. All these sounds imitate two bucks pushing each other around.

After such a sequence plus, perhaps, one more bit of tine rattling, rest a bit. In two to five minutes, go over it again, varying the routine any way you wish. You can't go too far wrong. If you see a deer coming and you are well hidden, you can often bring it right to you by very quietly "tickling" the tines together. At any rate, don't bang and rattle loudly when a buck is in sight and coming in. Occasionally I have brought in a reluctant or especially cautious buck simply by raking gravel a bit. You don't have to go through the gravel and bark raking and bush beating, but it certainly adds to the illusion.

If you will have faith in rattling, and stay with it, trying it during the rut and concentrating your efforts on still, crisp dawns, you will eventually bring a buck in, and maybe many of them. Once you do, I can promise that you'll be hooked. Many hunters just cannot believe this works. The first time you have a big old trophy buck practically trying to get into the thicket with you where you're hiding, you may wish for a few moments that it didn't work quite so well!

9

Elk and Moose

AMONG THOSE WHO have had the experience, there is a saying that no sportsman has been elk or moose hunting until he has called up a big bull within a few yards. This is certainly true. Of the two animals, elk are to some extent more susceptible to calling because they are more vocal. Let me tell an anecdote about what the experience is like.

Ted Burt, chief of law enforcement for the New Mexico Game and Fish Department, is an expert elk caller. I was with him several years ago in the high country of northern New Mexico just prior to the season for mature bulls, which falls always during the rut. We were going to try for live-elk photos for several days, and then begin a hunt. I was on a magazine assignment.

One day we spotted a lone bull off in a meadow "bugling" every few minutes. A bull without a harem is always in a mean and frustrated mood. He probably has been whipped by some other bull, and he is crazed to find cows and ready to fight other bulls. We made a sneak on the elk, staying in timber that brought us out on a narrow point overlooking the mountain meadow. We lay down among the trees. Ted some yards behind me. I had only a camera with a 300 mm. telephoto lens as my prime "weapon."

The instant Ted blew his "elk whistle" the bull whirled and replied. Then it came trotting down and across the meadow. Ted called again, the bull answered, and this process was repeated. Meanwhile I had focused and was shooting color photos as fast as I could. In my intentness and concentration I finally realized that I could not now get the head of the elk, with antlers, into the frame even when I turned the camera to a vertical position. I eased the camera down from my eye—and was startled to find that the animal was no more that fifteen paces from me.

The author watches while Ted Burt works on a bull. Burt, a New Mexican elk-calling expert, makes his calls from electrical conduit, which he then wraps with tape.

A big bull elk so aroused is a sight indeed. Its hackles were raised, its eyes wild. It slobbered, it was caked with mud from wallowing — a habit during rut — and smelled terrible from urinating on its own hocks. When it wound up and screamed, my hair must have raised my cap. And when I shot another photo the animal could hear the shutter and though puzzled, it seemed to mean business. It began a slow stalk around the end of the point, wary but ready to fight. I was not certain whether to lie closer to ground, or try running and making a go at climbing a tree.

Ted, some distance behind me and realizing there was some danger, whistled again, softly, to take the bull's attention from me. It began to stalk the sound and as it came around to my left a small breeze took human scent to it. Its expression was one of astonishment mingled with rage. Suddenly it wheeled and raced back around and up the meadow. Still, it paused twice to hurl back a challenge at us.

ELK BASICS

Whether or not you hunt, calling elk as you can well understand from the above, can be a thrilling experience. It is the perfect way to collect photos at close range. It is not always that easy. But when a bull makes up its mind to come in, the action may be fast and dramatic. Bull elk can be called only during the rut. The elk is an animal that collects a harem, from half a dozen to as many as forty or more cows. Mature bulls keep their harems under control, circling, prodding the cows to drive them ahead, bugling both to attract more cows and to challenge other bulls.

The rut—the chief portion of it—generally lasts for only two or three weeks, although it may be strung out somewhat longer. During this concentrated period, activity among the animals is at fever pitch. Young bulls hang around the herd fringes, harassing the herd bulls, sneaking in to try to run off cows. Fights are common. A deposed old herd bull may be wary about coming to a call after having been soundly whipped. By the end of the rut the big active bulls are gaunt and barely able sometimes to stagger along. Thus, if you intend to hunt by calling a bull for meat, it is important to do so, given open season, as soon as the rut starts, before the bulls become thin and smelly and practically unfit to eat.

Over the fairly broad range of elk, from portions of Arizona up through the Rockies and the northwest and British Columbia, timing of the rut will differ some. Weather during any given fall will also influence the timing. If it is unseasonably warm, the rut may come a bit later. By and large, however, the middle of September to the middle of October will catch about all of it. Although you should check for the amount of elk sign in a given area —tracks, droppings, rubs, wallows—you will know how abundant elk are by simply listening.

Bugling generally begins at or before dawn. It continues on well into the morning. Individual bulls will differ in their timing. Some without cows or with few cows may continue to bugle most of the morning. But the bulk of the bugling activity will occur from dawn until mid-morning. By then the breeding bulls will be bushed and all the elk will begin to move or will have moved out of the meadows and their fringes where much of the activity takes place, back into the timber to lie down. By mid to late afternoon bugling will begin again. Sometimes the peak is very late, the hour prior to and during dusk.

Elk are likely to be high up during the rut because the weather is just pleasantly crisp, and storms have not yet driven them to lower elevations.

Once you are in elk country, you won't have to read any books to know the bugle of an elk when you hear it. The sound carries far. At a distance it sounds almost musical, a whistling scream that starts low and ascends several octaves. Close up the sound is quite different and very startling. It begins with a low rasping, grating sound deep in the throat. The bull's head and neck are extended. The bugle immediately rises in both volume and pitch, running up the scale to end and fall off in a high-pitched scream. This is followed by a series of guttural grunts and coughs.

You shouldn't attempt to imitate these. In fact, an elk "whistle" listened to at close range does not really sound like the elk at all. It imitates only the ascending portion of the bugle, it is not as loud, and it is much thinner, more reedy. Yet it carries a long distance and to a bull sounds like another bull challenging at a distance.

There are a number of good elk calls available. Some are made of plastic, some of wood. They are usually about twelve to fourteen inches long. Some

The chief portion of the rut generally lasts only two or three weeks. By the end of this period the big active bulls, like this one, are gaunt and sometimes seem barely able to stagger along.

"take down" into two pieces for easier carrying. Many a homemade elk whistle has been fashioned from a length of metal electrical conduit about a half-inch in diameter, covered with tape so it doesn't clank against anything. It is fashioned like a regular whistle, with a *V* notch cut in near the blowing end. Beginners should use a commercially made call, however, for these are, in general, carefully researched to produce the correct tone.

Some calls have flute-like holes which are closed by the fingers at the beginning of the whistle and then progressively raised to ascend the scale. Some callers accomplish this by cupping the hand around the far end of the call to begin and then progressively opening it. The caller begins blowing easily, then increases the force of his breath. Easy to follow instructions are packed with elk calls, and these, coupled with the experience gained by listening to the elk and imitating them will soon have the caller calling perfectly. The fact is, elk calling is not especially difficult. During the rut, particularly, the bulls are crazed by desire, and they don't always listen for your mistakes!

CALLING ELK

One important point for beginning elk callers to understand is that bull voices differ a great deal among individuals, and especially among age groups. The bugle of the spike bull — the young bull — is thin and reedy and shrill. You can easily spot these just by careful listening. The bulls with the grating, raspy voices followed by raucous coughing grunts, are the old-timers. They scream with a jolting sound, then a ratchety *EEOUGHHH, YOWK, YOWK, YOWK,* that at close range sets one's teeth on edge, almost like the bray of a jackass.

Probably your call will not sound so rasping. In fact, it's not supposed to. Most call manufacturers attempt to get a sound that resembles the spike, and not the old bull. Thus the timbre of the call is thin. The reason for this is simple. Young bulls are always eager and fiddling around a herd fringe. Nothing infuriates a mature bull more than the presence, and sounds, of pipsqueak youngsters with the gall to try cutting in. Quite often a big old bull will scream back at matching bulls in nearby timber or in the same meadow where he holds his harem. But he probably won't leave the cows to go after the big boy. Yet a spike bugling nearby may cause the old herd bull to answer and take off on the run.

For best results, begin calling at or before dawn and continue into midmorning. By then the breeding bulls are bushed and move back into timber. Bugling resumes by mid to late afternoon and may peak at dusk. Bulls without cows or with only a few may call most of the morning. The author here blows a call fashioned from plastic tubing.

It is of course always the lone bull that is most likely to come to a call. Sometimes spikes are easy to call, but not always. This is not so much a matter of wariness as timidity. The lone, mature bull is the one with confidence, unless he has been too soundly whipped by another bull. Even then, the reedy sound of a call that seems to him to be a spike may impress him as easy pickings, and he'll respond. A caller must realize that a bull with a harem will probably bugle constantly, and will usually answer a call. But it won't necessarily *come* to the call. If you are calling and the answers are repeated but never come closer, you are probably dealing with a bull that has cows with him.

This bull is fairly easy to stalk. Get its position, keep to timber, watch the wind, and move in slowly. Call every now and then. If the answers stay in relatively the same area, a cautious approach may put the whole band in sight, and range. One of the biggest bulls I ever saw we stalked in this fashion. We had him in sight at long range for half an hour. He had a large band of cows. The bull answered the caller with wild, screaming bugles, but would not leave the group. The hunter started a stalk, keeping to a strip of timber, while the caller continued from the same spot in order to retain the attention of the bull, and to keep the hunter on course. He collected the big bull at less than forty yards!

While bulls battle over harems, the cows will watch the fight. The winning bull then herds all the gals away.

You cannot be certain, of course, that the answering bull has cows with him. Some animals will constantly reply but won't come in, yet are alone. You can stalk these, too. In a film a partner and I produced one year for Remington Arms and Redfield Scope, we operated on and collected just such a bull. When we were about one hundred yards from it, we still had not seen it. A final whistle brought the bull out of timber into the open. He was a curious and an immobile target caught by both camera and gun. If you are calling however, and an answering bull gets farther and farther away, you may as well forget it. Even at a walk elk move swiftly, and one headed in a certain direction, still bugling, undoubtedly is with his cows or has other things in mind.

When calling, you should always keep an alert watch. Now and then a bull moves in on you without a sound. Ted Burt, mentioned at the beginning of this chapter, had an enormous bull suddenly show so close to him that Ted could not tell through his scope where he was aiming. All he could see was hair. This bull had come in without a single bugle. The usual reason for this is that the elk, ordinarily a large one, is just past his prime. He can't quite hack it with the more vigorous mature bulls. Yet there is always a chance that he can sneak in and coax a straggler cow away, without getting into a fight. And incidentally, if you are new at observing elk and have the idea that those enormous antlers are bound to make a racket as the bull moves through timber, get it out of your mind. It is uncanny how silently a huge-racked bull can slip through dense timber.

Individual bulls may bugle in differing patterns. The more furious period, particularly if elk are abundant and competition is severe, is at dawn and an hour or so after. But periods between bugles will vary with different animals. Don't try to press a bull too hard. If you get a reply, wait a few seconds or a minute before you whistle again. In new territory, get on a ridge and listen. If the rut is on and no elk are sounding off, you'd better move. If you hear a distant bull, don't call until you have moved within three to five hundred yards of him. This way the next calls can bring the bull into range. Always be exceedingly quiet in elk country, in your camp, riding a horse, or prowling. Elk are very easily disturbed, and when they move they may go for miles.

If you intend to become an elk caller, it's best to make a point of getting into your territory and setting up your camp some days before season. If possible, get back far away from any crowd of hunters that may disturb the animals. And as I've said, be quiet around camp. Set up well away from the main herds that you hear. Then get out and listen, without any calling. Learn what bull elk sound like, what different age groups sound like. Locate the bailiwicks of several good bulls. They may wander, but if they have cows they may stay within a square mile, and sometimes less.

If you happen to sit down to call, and suddenly realize that two bulls are bugling, one on either side, don't make a sound. Just listen. Often they'll start approaching each other and will practically run over you en route.

I have mentioned stalking and whistling at a bull that will answer but won't come to you. A good trick here, on occasion, is to move in a little way, enough so it's obvious your whistle is nearer to the bull, and then pause a bit. Then move in again. Don't call too much. Bulls uncannily pinpoint each other. If you call as if you are a shy but rut-crazed spike, even a reluctant mature bull can seldom stand it. He may suddenly come on the run.

KEY RULES FOR ELK CALLING

Basics for beginning elk callers are as follows. Don't worry about whether or not you'll recognize the bugling of elk when you hear it. It is the only such sound in nature, and it is so unique that it is unmistakable. When you make your setup, or stand, arrange it so you can see well. Most elk range is a combination of timber, such as aspen and spruce and pine, with scattered openings or mountain meadows. Elk hide and rest in the timber, but consort daily in the meadows or along their fringes. Like any other animal, elk will circle to get the wind on the caller, if there is a breeze. So your stand, and your watch, should take this into consideration. Still, frosty clear mornings are always best. Fog and drizzle inhibit activity to some extent. Most of the time it is the elk up on a slope that responds best to a call, moving downslope. Bulls in a valley are somewhat reluctant to move up. However, this is not an infallible rule, but you should consider it at least, to give yourself every break.

MOOSE BASICS

Not many hunters or photographers have ever attempted to call moose. Moose calling has been practiced by guides, chiefly in Canada, for many years. It was a common method used also by Indians. Like elk calling and rattling deer, it is based upon the rut period. The rut may start as early as mid-September and run in some areas into late November. The peak of rut is generally during October.

The personalities of moose are quite different from those of elk or deer. They are on the whole rather sedentary animals. Even the period of the rut, although filled with high agitation, is by no means pitched to as high a level as elk and deer. Unlike elk, moose do not gather a harem. A bull seeks one cow at a time. He may spend a few days with her and then seek another.

Moose are not as vocal as elk, and during the rut it is the cow that utters the most sounds. Ugly as she is, she's a real vamp, running in circles, bawling with hoarse calls to attract a bull. Bulls may at this time utter deep, coarse grunts. They also rip their massive antlers through bushes and against trees. A bull moose can move as quietly as an elk through timber, but during the rut he is likely to crash around, especially when he hears the grunting of another bull or the pleading call of the cow.

During rut, cow moose do most of the calling. A bull accepts the invitation and stays with a single cow for a few days. Here, a mechanical cow call (between man and bull) doesn't quite measure up to the bull's expectations.

At this time royal battles may develop between powerful bulls. Young bulls, however, think twice about mixing it with a big one. In fact, moose are more interested in breeding than fighting, probably due to the lack of a harem system. It is thus easier for each bull to find a cow with which to consort.

CALLING MOOSE

The problem for a would-be moose caller is that he is not very likely to hear enough moose talk—or any—by which to learn to imitate the sounds. Because of their size, moose are scattered, seldom concentrated. The chance of hearing a cow or a grunting bull is slim. This is why guides, who've lived long in moose country, have generally done the calling. The classic caller is the Indian guide who fashions a birchbark megaphone through which he imitates the *ugh-waugh, ugh-waugh* of the cow.

Some guides work out a routine with the opposite tack. They imitate the grunts of a bull, and meanwhile crash a heavy stick against bushes and trees. From a canoe, the grunting call may also be accompanied with sloshing paddle sounds to mimic a wading bull. Another classic method, often recounted in hunting literature, combines the use of the birchbark horn to simulate the wailing cow, and a simultaneous, or following, hatful or bucketful of water poured or dribbled over the side of the canoe. The water sounds like a cow urinating in a lake. It is obvious that too much repetition of this technique would only arouse suspicion in a bull. Dawn and particularly dusk are the best moose calling times.

Probably moose calling will never be as popular as calling elk or deer, because fewer hunters have the opportunity to hunt moose. But the fact is, calling moose is very effective during the rut, if you are within a bull's hearing range. And today substantial advances have been made in moose calling. There are several instructional records available so that a would-be moose caller can listen to either the actual recorded sounds, or to excellent simulations.

As an example, one such record, advertised by Herter's of Waseca, Minnesota, lists the following calls in their catalog: "Side One tells how and when to use the common moose horn. The horn can be made of birchbark, cardboard, tar paper or any such material. Side One also gives calls and instructions to reproduce calls of: 1. Cow looking for bull moose. 2. Bull answering from far off. 3. Bull answering when close. 4. Bull call in search of cow. 5. Calf in search of cow. 6. Cow answer to lost calf moose. 7. How to imitate cow walking in water. 8. How to imitate cow urinating in water."

That gives you an idea of how easily one may learn moose calls. Further, there are calling records for use in the field. In fact, Side 2 on the record above is designed for field use. I have listened to it but have not tried yet.

A recent development which will be of great interest to prospective moose callers is that of Johnny Stewart (Johnny Stewart Game Calls, Box 7594, Waco, Texas 76710). For some years Stewart has marketed various recorded calls—first records, and then cassette tapes. He phoned me from way up in the Rockies some months ago while I was writing this book and was very excited over a new moose tape he had developed. He had his family with him, and he told me his oldest daughter and another girl had called eight moose in three days. Later I discussed this phenomenon with Johnny. The tape was scheduled to be available by spring 1975.

A few other taped or recorded moose calls are available. So far as I know, however, there is no mouth-operated moose call made, and, with the recording developments, none really is needed.

How you make your stand for moose calling depends on where you hunt. In the few Rockies states where moose range, they are mountain animals. Just sitting and glassing to find one on a slope or in a valley may be successful. It may be necessary to move in and try the call. You can set up in a valley where there is moose sign, and play the call. In terrain such as in Ontario, for example, where moose are abundant, the animals stay in rather dense timber, but commonly feed along pond, lake, and river edges. You can make a stand in brush near a pond wherever there is much sign. This, however, does not allow much maneuvering. When calling from a canoe, and listening for replies or a crashing bull, you can quickly get into position either to hide or to intercept the animal.

In northwestern Canada where large expanses of open uplands are broken with strips of timber and brush, hunters on horseback often spot moose at great distances. Granted, the animals can usually be stalked successfully without the use of a call. But enticing a huge bull to you either with sounds of a lovesick cow or with grunts of a challenging bull is certainly a unique and interesting experience. Calling moose can bring sensational results for the hunter and the photographer as well.

10

Antelope, Caribou and Javelina

As ALL ASTUTE OBSERVERS of wildlife know, the type of terrain in which an animal lives has a direct bearing upon which of its senses are the most acute and most used. Whitetail deer, always in cover or its fringes, see and hear well but their highly developed sense of smell is their primary bulwark against danger. The pronghorn, or antelope, lives on the wide-open, nearly treeless plains. It does not even like to venture into patches of cover taller than itself. It cannot see out from such places. It depends on its sight and fleetness for safety.

It may seem odd to many readers, especially experienced big game hunters, to speak of "calling" antelope. In fact, the three big-game animals covered in this chapter are almost never called. But they *can* be, and that is why I discuss them in this book. Each type of calling is an intriguing and unique endeavor, whether for hunting, for photography, or just for fun.

ANTELOPE

The eyes of an antelope are set much farther out at the sides of its head than are those of members of the deer family. It is interesting to note also that antelope eyes are larger than those of a horse, even though the average antelope seldom weighs more than a tenth as much. The size and location of its eyes give the antelope an unusually wide range of vision. Whether right or not, some experts claim that the eyes have a binocular ability. At any rate, mark well that the reason for this heightened eye development is the lack of cover in antelope habitat. With its eyes to give warning, the antelope can spot any possible danger at great distance and, instead of hiding, take flight. The antelope is the swiftest hoofed animal on the continent.

Invariably, animals with exceptional eyesight are also extremely curious. This curiosity has saved the life of—and also has been the downfall of—many an antelope and is the trait appealed to by the caller. When antelope spot something at a great distance that they are not quite sure of, they puzzle over it. Antelope have learned through experience that a man walking or a pickup truck kicking up dust is possible danger. But an unusual sight that cannot be easily identified arouses their innate curiosity. If this unidentified phenomenon stays in the same place, antelope almost without fail, will move toward it, closer and closer until identifying it. If antelope can't make out what they see even at a hundred yards, sometimes they will come right on in—to extremely close range.

Early plains hunters, both Indians and whites, understood the habits of the antelope through observation, and they used this knowledge to their advantage. Indians crawled along a shallow gully to a patch of high sage, and tied a bunch of feathers to the top of a bush. The feathers, on a light thong, streamed out into the ever-active breeze on the plains and could be

Taking advantage of the antelope's curiosity and keen eyesight, this hunter has brought a few animals up 200 yards by slowly waving his handkerchief.

seen from a great distance. The plains habitat is exceedingly sparse in character. Thus antelope bands, knowing every rock and sage clump in their domain, and well acquainted with other wild creatures with whom they shared it, were immediately puzzled to see this odd and stationary fluttering. Observing it for some minutes, they then began walking toward it. I suppose it is proper to say they were "tolled" rather than "called." The Indian, hiding flat to the ground with his bow in the sage, patiently waited for the antelope to come close enough for a shot.

Pioneers on the plains concocted all kinds of tricks for tolling antelope, which were fabulously abundant, and a prime source of meat. I recall reading of instances when a white rag was tied to a bush or, when there were no bushes, to a tall stake forced into the ground. The hunter lay in a gully watching. Sooner or later antelope would spot the fluttering cloth and move in. Another account relates how a hunter crawled to a low ridge top, spotted an antelope band, lay on his back and kicked his feet in the air. This brought them within easy range.

On numerous occasions I have succeeded in bringing antelope to me. As many a hunter and photographer knows, it is difficult to get close enough for shots, and making a stalk in antelope country is seldom easy. Thus tolling the animals into range can be useful as well as exciting. A few years ago I was making a film for GMC Truck, an antelope hunting film in which I was the actor-hunter. The cameraman was able to get ample live footage of the animals by using long telephoto lenses. But the problem we had was trying to get me in focus in the foreground, in the same frame with the antelope, or even with a single buck in focus at a distance. We couldn't sneak up on any of the animals that close, and of course having two people —the cameraman and myself—made the approach all the more difficult.

Finally easing to a ridgetop, we spotted a fair buck at an estimated three hundred yards. He had already noticed movement, but because we were lying down, having crawled up the ridge, he didn't know what we were. I suggested that the cameraman crawl off some yards behind me where he could get both me and the antelope in the frame. I was wearing a broad brimmed western hat. When the cameraman was all set, I sat up and began waving my hat in the air. After a wave or two, I pulled it down out of sight, and I hunched over. In a couple of minutes, I repeated the action.

The buck stared at first, then began walking slowly toward us. The closer he came, the more mesmerized he appeared to be. When he was about a hundred yards out, I didn't sit erect any more, but only waved the hat. At an estimated seventy-five yards I heard the camera start, sat up and raised my rifle, and we had all the film footage of a successfully concluded hunt.

This is roughly the technique I have used several times. If the animals see you and identify you properly before you hide and wave at them, they are usually too suspicious to move in. But if you are sitting or crawling when they first see you, they are not likely to make a correct identification.

On another occasion, while producing a film for Remington Arms and simultaneously working on a magazine assignment for *Outdoor Life,* I had one of the characters in the project wave a big hat from behind a rock, and also raise and lower it atop his rifle barrel. This brought a buck to us. The same man, right out on grassy plains, brought two other bucks within fifty yards by lying in the grass and waving a white handkerchief.

Sometimes a similar trick will work to get a running antelope to stop and look. I was in northeastern New Mexico filming another hunt. We had seen an exceptional buck several times, but always he had eluded us. On this rather story-book occasion—the last hours of the last day of the season, with the film all wrapped up except for footage of collecting a buck—we were driving a ranch trail when we saw a buck with some does in a small basin.

Not vocal animals themselves, antelope sometimes respond to basic predator calls. This group appeared over the ridge to investigate the author's call.

They immediately ran up into the bordering hills, which were covered with malpai hummocks—actually black volcanic rock. We raced with the vehicle down into the basin. Then the cameraman and I jumped out and took off into the hills. For some reason the antelope had circled partly back. We caught sight of them at long range, running obliquely away. The cameraman, with a tripod and long lens, instantly got on them and I heard the camera whirr. I of course was not in the frame but we desperately needed that buck or our project would have been nothing. I dropped behind a hummock of rock, took a quick rest, pulled off my hat and frantically waved it. The buck stopped instantly, whirled and looked straight at us. He was an exceedingly narrow target at probably 375 yards, but somehow or other I downed him, and we had the whole sequence "in the can."

If you try this tolling, don't always expect such dramatic results. During the closed season when the bands are not disturbed, they respond quite well. Lone trophy bucks—old fellows—are likely to be wary at any time. After hunting season opens, in any area where the animals are choused around for a few days, they become wild as hawks and hard to fool. Nonetheless, bringing in antelope in this manner—however you elect to try it—is often successful enough to make it a standard part of your hunting lore.

ANTELOPE SOUNDS

Few hunters realize it, but the curiosity of antelope can be aroused with a predator call. I related earlier how mule deer will come to this sound. Antelope occasionally react the same way. What they imagine the sound is, no one can say. Possibly they believe one of their own kind is in distress. The only sound I have ever heard an antelope make is the short *blatt* of a buck in rut, and once that of a wounded buck. But this is an uncommon sound. These are not very vocal creatures. To experiment with a predator call, you must hide just as you would if calling coyotes on the plains. In fact, that's what you may call up instead of antelope! But if you can spot a band without their seeing you, quite often they will respond to the sound.

CARIBOU

Caribou are also curious animals. They are far more naive than antelope, however, and sometimes act as if they are not very intelligent. Not a great many hunters experience caribou hunting nowadays, and they're often first-timers at it. But knowing that caribou can be tolled closer, in the same manner as antelope, can be valuable information.

I recall an amusing incident related to me by a fellow who had just returned from his first caribou hunt. He and his guide had located an exceptional bull. It was too far away for a shot, so the guide suggested that the hunter make a stalk. There was very little cover. Since two would be more conspicuous than one, the guide told the hunter to go it alone. The guide, well hidden, was able to watch the comic scene.

The hunter hunched over, and gained a hundred yards before the bull was alerted. At the bull's first sign of awareness, the hunter dropped to all fours. The bull stood, staring. The hunter kept down and began crawling. As the fellow related it to me, he said he purposely kept his face down and didn't look, hoping to get closer and have the bull stay put. When he did peek again, he was amazed at how far he had crawled. The caribou was not over sixty yards from him. Then the fellow noticed that the animal had been moving toward *him* at the same time and didn't know what this "thing" was, and was curious. Before the fellow realized what was happening, the

By far, not the smartest species in the deer family, caribou, such as this barren ground bull, can be tolled in with a variety of caller movements that don't betray the normal, upright human form.

caribou started trotting right at him. He raised up, it stopped, stared incredulously, and he collected his trophy.

Guides have brought caribou closer by hat waving and various antics comparable to the antelope routine. It doesn't always work. But it is worth trying when the situation demands.

JAVELINA

Last on the list of hoofed big-game animals that respond to a call is the javelina. Perhaps it is even questionable if these odd little desert pigs are "big" game. They average only thirty-five to forty pounds, an exceptional animal weighs more than fifty pounds. Because of the javelina's rather restricted range, many hunters have never hunted or even seen one. They make appealing trophies. Within the United States they are found in Texas, New Mexico, and Arizona. Texas has the largest number, and Arizona is second. They are also abundant in parts of Mexico.

Javelina respond to basic predator calls. This one, having approached within 15 feet of the author, raises his snout to get scent.

There is no javelina call marketed. But a few years ago, a number of varmint, or predator, callers within javelina range discovered that the animal would often respond to the standard coyote or fox call. If you are acquainted with javelina, you know that they may have young at any time of year, but no more than two young are born at a time. The piglets squeal in a high-pitched voice and are sometimes quite noisy. Mature javelina grunt, and when aroused pop their teeth together in a most menacing—but usually bluffing—manner. When they run away because of danger they make a *chuff-chuff-chuff* sound.

It is possible that javelina hear a predator call as the distress cry of a piglet. Though they are chiefly vegetarians, they are known to eat carrion, and on occasion may kill small or injured animals, and eat them. Conceivably, javelina may come to a predator squall hoping to catch some injured rabbit. Whatever their reason for responding, it must be admitted that nothing is very predictable about them. I was with Murry Burnham late one afternoon when we sat down to try to call a coyote in the south-Texas Brush Country. Immediately we heard a rattle of small gravel and a popping of brush. Two javelina came running out to within thirty feet or so of us.

The eyesight of the javelina is very poor. Much of the time it hardly seems to know what it is looking at. Its sense of hearing is good enough, but it is not always frightened by sounds. However, its nose is excellent, and once it gets your scent it is usually long gone, into the brush or down some winding desert gully. The two pigs above had their noses stretched high, trying to make out what we were. Camouflaged, we sat with our backs to a bush.

I should point out here that Murry was armed with bow and arrow. Bow hunters can use calls of all kinds to special advantage, and they have used the predator call often, in Arizona especially, when trying to collect javelina. At any rate, these two pigs came closer and closer. Suddenly they knew things were not right. Their hackles raised. A javelina with its long neck bristles upended in alarm looks as if it weighs four times what it actually does. One whirled and went "chuffing" and bounding away. The other popped its teeth and eyed us for several minutes, circling stiff legged, as if it had a notion to take us on.

These two javelina don't know what to make of the anguished cries coming from the amplifier. Note the photographer in the background.

There are no known specialized techniques for calling javelinas, probably because you never know whether or not they will respond. In open country such as that in the Big Bend region of Texas, an area of desert mountains, javelina can be spotted quite regularly at long range. Some callers have brought in singles, or couples, right to them by hiding and blowing a coyote call just as they would for coyotes. A high-pitched call seems most effective. In dense cover such as that of southern Texas, the difficulty in hunting javelina is getting to see them. They might be quite close but hidden in the cactus and thornbrush. Calling here sometimes brings them into the open, such as a ranch trail or an open area surrounding a ranch tank or waterhole.

At other times, I have watched a band and blown the predator call without getting any response at all—they just kept right on traveling. Usually their response is to come in as if prepared to fight, hackles up and teeth chattering. Some callers who've been successful believe that a band that has young piglets in it is more likely to be influenced than those without. I listened with amusement last year to a fellow who had never had experience with javelina and who was trying to call up a coyote. He found himself suddenly all but surrounded by a band of pigs, all chattering and acting mighty evil in intent.

I've never known them to do anything but bluff, unless cornered. Their sharp dog teeth, in both lower and upper jaw, are capable of inflicting severe damage, however. The caller was plenty scared. He fired off his rifle as fast as he could, jumped up and looked wildly about for a tree to climb. In that cactus and brush country there were none. By the time he realized it, every pig had fled. And when he checked to see how many he'd killed, he discovered he hadn't hit a single one!

As I stated early in this book, there probably is no creature that cannot be called somehow. The animals in this chapter are good arguments for the case.

11

Squirrels

THERE IS AN old hunting joke that goes: "How do you call a squirrel? Climb up a tree, and make like a nut!"

Oddly enough, it's no joke at all. Squirrels have been called that way. For example, where squirrels are actively feeding on nuts — such as beech nuts in the hull and still on the tree, or on green pecans and other green or nearly ripe nuts hanging on branches — they scurry along a limb, reach out, get a nut, and then begin to husk it. They drop the outer covering and pieces of shell that they snip off. Squirrels cut twigs and drop them when they are feeding on buds. Many an old-time squirrel hunter has located his quarry by sitting quietly in the woods listening for the sound of falling "cuttings" as they rustle upon dry leaves.

From this, the hunter can imitate the sound of squirrels dropping shells and twigs — with occasional success. I knew an old man who dearly loved to hunt squirrels and had been hunting them for fifty years. I hunted with him one day in a quiet woodlot. After stealing unobtrusively into the woods, we had found a big beech tree and had hidden near it in low cover. He took from his pocket a handful of small pebbles. He waited, pebbles in hand, for a full ten minutes. And then, making no motions, he began shooting them out by laying one on a forefinger and popping it with his thumb.

As each tiny pebble dropped, it made a dry rattle on leaves. After a dozen or so in quick succession, we heard the soft *chuckle* of a squirrel off at a distance. It sounded high up. He nudged me and indicated I should keep an eye peeled up in high branches. Presently I saw a branch flip down and then up. But there was no breeze. A squirrel had caused the motion and was coming. The old hunter flipped out pebbles steadily. The silent woods emphasized the small sounds, and the squirrel had obviously heard them. Here the animal undoubtedly envisioned a bonanza of food where another or several squirrels were feeding, but not talking about it. In due time the squirrel, a big fox squirrel, came scurrying along a limb within gun range, and was brought to bag.

Although that kind of "calling" illustrates the authenticity of the old joke, it isn't a usual method of calling squirrels. The most effective method is the use of a squirrel call to imitate the barks and other "talk" of squirrels. A substantial number of hunters already practice squirrel calling, but they are still a minority. The fact is, squirrel calling is one of the most sporting and intriguing methods of squirrel hunting and is abundantly successful. It is also an extremely important ruse for photographers and observers of wildlife.

Of course hunters are the people most interested in squirrels. This animal is second only to the cottontail as our most popular small-game target. In average years in this country, at least twenty million squirrels are harvested, and put on the dinner tables. Yet the harvest only dents the squirrel population. These animals are cyclic. They build up fantastic populations for a few years, and then, probably because of their own fecundity, plunge to levels that seem, to locals, near extinction. Yet they always bounce back—given proper habitat and food.

Even though habitat is quite obviously the prime requisite, the abundance of food is undoubtedly the factor controlling the squirrel populations. For example, in areas such as the Ozarks, when weather conditions are amenable to a high squirrel production and to the production of food such as acorns, extremely high squirrel populations occur. But the very fact of super abundance strains the food supply. And then if, in the following season wild food production is low, the squirrel population plummets.

Tom May, a game warden friend of mine in Van Buren, a village in the Missouri Ozarks in the center of a vast forest region of superb habitat for gray squirrels, related to me that he had arrested three hunters who had set up a camp back in the woods and been in it two and one-half days. They had in possession at that time 323 gray squirrels! An incident such as this may give a prospective squirrel caller better insight into understanding why he may do well one season and poorly the next.

Tom also told me of another season when the squirrels were so plentiful that they had cleaned up every bit of food by early fall. They began "migrating" by the thousands across the Current River, now in the National Scenic River system. This river is a fairly large, swift, clear stream flowing through the forested hills in the area and was so full of squirrels swimming across it, undoubtedly looking for new foraging areas, that had it been legal to do so Tom could have floated a boat down it and in minutes scooped up a limit in a landing net. There are many such tales of these enormous movements throughout history.

The following fall I spent some time there, and was in the woods and driving back-trails every day. In a full week we didn't see a single squirrel. I

Since gray squirrels rise early, one of the best talking times is at dawn.

Fox squirrels may be out at dawn but tend to be late-sleepers. Both gray and fox squirrels feed heavily until dusk.

The tassel-eared Kaibab squirrel, here, is found only on the north rim of the Grand Canyon and is protected. Its relative, the Abert squirrel, is huntable and ranges in the forests of Colorado, New Mexico and Arizona.

135

talked to a number of hunters. They were getting very few. Most didn't bother to hunt the animals because they knew what happened after such peak cycles. There had obviously been a tremendous winter die-off. Knowledge of the population cycle of squirrels helps tyro squirrel callers understand why results may be excellent one year and poor the next.

TECHNIQUES FOR CALLING SQUIRRELS

There are two main groups of game squirrels, the fox squirrels and the gray squirrels. Each has subspecies and color phases. The fox squirrel is the larger of the two, but squirrel sizes differ drastically from place to place. It is fairly common in some northern and eastern locations for fox squirrels to weigh two or even three pounds. Gray squirrels at maximum weigh slightly over a pound. In some places they are smaller. Southerners call the grays "cat" squirrels.

Old hands know precisely where to find each variety, but beginners should be aware that the grays are basically creatures of the forest. The fox squirrels are animals of farm woodlots and more open woodlands – open groves or dry ridges where openings are found among the trees. They also live in well-drained valleys and along stream courses, but the grays may be in swamps. In some places in the South grays are even hunted from boats gliding among stands of cypress.

The two varieties are occasionally found in the same locations. The region I mentioned a moment ago, the Missouri Ozarks, has good populations of both types of squirrel. The larger fox squirrels are generally found in big timber along the stream courses and on farm fringes, the grays almost anywhere in the forest.

Squirrel calling is used primarily to persuade a squirrel to expose its whereabouts. On many occasions a squirrel will reply but will not come to the call. A careful hunter then makes a short stalk, remaining hidden behind tree trunks, before calling again. With luck he is able to spot his quarry. Sometimes squirrels do not reply, but after hearing the sound of the call they might come out of hiding or try to get into a position to see where the sound is coming from. The hunter should watch every moment. The slightest movement of a branch, the flick of a tail, a head peeking around a trunk gives away the position of his quarry.

However, squirrels also come to calls, at times from amazing distances. Some individuals apparently are aroused to anger by hearing another squirrel in the vicinity. These squirrels may reply with loud, angry barking, and travel clear across a woodlot to see what's going on, chattering all the way. Conversely, other individuals come without a sound. I have had the experience of hiding at the base of a large tree, calling every few minutes for half an hour, and suddenly hearing a squirrel leap branch to branch into the tree against which I was sitting. On one such occasion, a large fox squirrel came down the trunk almost to the top of my camouflage cap and net.

Nowadays a number of states have open season on squirrels early in fall, when foliage is still dense. A substantial number of states also have spring seasons, falling in May, June or July, after the young are well grown. At this time foliage is also dense. These are the times when calling is most useful. A hunter simply prowling the woods puts every squirrel into hiding. But if he quietly enters, sits down and uses his call, he can bring squirrels into exposure that he would never otherwise have known were there.

It is important to understand the differences in personality between fox and gray squirrels. The gray, fundamentally a forest animal, is invariably much wilder. If you walk under a tree in which several fox squirrels are feeding and stand quietly trying to locate them, every one will lie close along a limb, hiding immobile until you move on. Try the same thing under a tree where gray squirrels are feeding and in seconds every one will flee wildly through the tree tops.

SQUIRREL SOUNDS

The vocabulary of squirrels is not large. In fact, the only sound a squirrel caller needs to perfect is the *kuk,* or *chuck,* which is ordinarily spoken of as "barking." However, there are several variations in patterns of this sound, that is, in the number and speed of the individual "barks." And there are also varying volume inflections, from a harsh, strident, angry tone, to a soft repetition that seems to speak of contentment.

It has been written many times that the bark of the fox squirrel is coarse and that the gray's is much softer. This is a little too pat. Squirrel voices are rather individual, differing among squirrels in any given place, and also from place to place. But a caller does not need to worry about this, for the squirrels themselves certainly realize it. The bark of the two varieties is really much the same, but often the big fox squirrels seem to be more reserved. This fits in with their hiding practices. They are not anxious to have their presence known. Conversely, gray squirrels may chatter and softly chuckle much more. Yet no rule can be set up. I have "talked" just for fun to a fox squirrel in my yard and aroused it to such annoyance that it incessantly chattered. It does the same when it sees a cat. Also, a big lone fox squirrel — usually an old male — may come across a grove toward the sound of a call, running on the ground, bounding into trees, barking all the way, tremendously agitated.

One of the best ways to learn to imitate squirrel chatter and to size up the meanings of inflections is to spend some time in parks where squirrels live and are reasonably gentle. From listening to them and being able to see them at the same time, you soon learn their reactions to the various volume and pattern differences. There are also instruction records available from several of the call manufacturers. These show you, and tell you, how your call should sound. Some records are made with just the calling portions — no recorded human voice instructions — so that if you wish you can play them on a mechanical caller out in the woods. For squirrel hunting, however, this is a little bit awkward, and you do not have the precise control that is possible when using a hand-operated call.

SQUIRREL CALLS

Over the years numerous types of squirrel calls have been marketed. The "striker" variety was the original. This kind of call is in two parts, a box or barrel resonator, and a striker. A few years ago I had one that was made of wood. The wooden barrel was held in the left hand. A thin, stiff piece of

Squirrel calls emit variations on the *kuk* or *chuck* sound referred to as barking. Each allows varieties of voice pattern, tempo, volume and inflection. Lower center is a squeeze bulb. Left is a box with metal plate, lip and striker. Next are a wood-to-wood striker and then a metal-to-metal striker. Right is the highly popular and easy-to-use bellows type.

hardwood thrust up from it. The striker was also of hardwood, with a saw-toothed edge. It was struck or scraped decisively across the top of the other thin piece, making a sound like the rasping bark of a squirrel. Another very popular model at that time was made with hard plastic outside, but with a brass striker which was struck against another edge of brass.

The striker calls have generally been replaced with other innovations. One, however, is still available, and popular. This is the Herter's call, which is interesting because with it you can match the tonal quality of individual squirrels. It is a walnut box with a brass plate or "reed" attached to the top. You can dash the knurled, rough steel striker against the edge of the brass plate to make the barking sounds. On the plate are six "X" marks in varied locations. By holding the thumb of the left hand on any one of these, you can make different tones.

The author shows the two-handed method of operating the metal-to-metal striker.

Most modern squirrel calls are based on the "squeeze bulb" principle. One kind, in fact, is simply a tiny rubber bulb with a "squeaker" in the neck end. When tapped against palm, gunstock or any other object, it mimics the chatter of a squirrel. Another—from Olt—is a plunger type. This one is fashioned from hard rubber. One end of the barrel contains a plunger. When tapped it also simulates the squirrel bark.

The close-up photo, left, shows how the hunter mutes the barrel end of a bellows call with his lower hand while tapping the rubber cap.

Undoubtedly the easiest calls for a beginner to use, and the most numerous ones nowadays, are what are called the "bellows" type. This variety has a wood or hard rubber barrel, to one end of which is attached a soft rubber or plastic bellows, the far end of the small bellows flattened. To operate it, you simply hold the barrel in one hand and tap the bellows end. By holding the bellows upright and cupping the hand around the lower end of the barrel, you can make various modulations, inflections and volumes. Or, the call can be turned over and the bellows simply tapped against gun stock or palm. The harder the tap, the louder and coarser the call.

The soft, quiet "chuckle" of a contented squirrel sounds something like this: *kukkukkukkukkukkukkuk,* the syllables run together and are given swiftly. But this should be done quietly, and somewhat muffled. One time, I sat in big lowland timber in spring, right in the middle of the afternoon, using this sound. Leaves and vines were dense. I kept utterly quiet and immobile, hiding behind a big downed log. About every three minutes I used just the chuckle, no loud barks. Presently there was the gentlest stirring of leaves above and in front of me, and a big fox squirrel peered silently out of a tangle of vines. I don't know if he had been in that tree all the time or if he had come to it.

More commonly used, either spring or fall, is a much harsher, louder sound. It has the first barks well spaced — sharp, strident, abrupt, emphatic and demanding — followed by a swift series. Here's a representation of it: *kuk — kuk — kuk — kukkukkukkukkukkuk.* Some callers believe in counting exact numbers of barks, and in working out precise series — for example, three long, sharp barks well spaced, followed by four short, swift ones. This is immediately followed by a similar series of two and four, and then with one and four. Incidentally, the short, swift series of barks is always made in diminishing volume, the way the animal makes them as it runs short of breath.

My personal opinion is that squirrels don't count the number of barks. Although exact routines certainly do no harm, I believe you can't go too far wrong making it all up as you go along. If you have heard a squirrel and intend to answer it, listen closely to the pattern it uses, and try to copy it.

When the woods are utterly silent, start out by giving a soft series. You can use the three or more spaced barks followed by the quick ones, but don't sound like an aroused squirrel. See what happens. If after several quiet tries you get a reply, it may be an angry one. If so, reply in kind. If the reply is gentle, call in the same manner. Keep in mind also that fox squirrels, except during mating season or when they find an especially appealing spot of forage, have little to do with each other. Conversely, grays often get along better among themselves.

Further, gray squirrels, like other forest animals, arise early. Often they are talking just before and during dawn. This is one of the very best calling times. Fox squirrels may be out at dawn, but they are more likely to sleep late. Late afternoon is a good calling time for both varieties. They feed heavily right up until dusk so they are comfortably full all night. On warm days squirrels hide and rest during midday, but you can still trick them into exposing themselves. A squirrel chattering at midday or early afternoon puzzles them, and their curiosity is aroused. On cool or overcast days squirrels often feed all day long.

Just as important as your calling technique is how quietly you operate while entering the territory and while calling. You must also remember not to call too much. The most successful callers wear full camouflage, even to headnet and gloves. It is a good idea to move into the woods *before* dawn. In fall, if you have located trees with an exceptional abundance of mast—a big beech, hickory, pecan, walnut—prowl silently in near it and hide yourself well. Begin calling softly just at dawn. Remain absolutely immobile and quiet—no cracking of sticks or hitching around. Sitting rather than standing, you won't be seen as easily.

In spring, a fruit bearing tree is a great place for a stand. As an example, wherever mulberry trees grow, seek the fruit bearing individual trees. Both gray and fox squirrels gorge on them. Take a stand nearby. It may even be in a farm field a full shotgun range away from the edge of a woods or timbered stream course. Call softly at dawn or in late afternoon from a place of proper concealment. Sometimes also the angry, strident call gets replies here, as if some crotchety old male wanted the place to himself. Don't be too hasty to try to collect the first squirrel that comes to such a bonanza of food. When the first squirrel appears, quit calling and remain utterly still. On one occasion I had a limit—five where I was hunting—three of them fox squirrels, two grays, all in the same tree at one time.

When you have taken a calling stand, regardless of time of day, remain quiet for ten or fifteen minutes before calling. If you hear a squirrel meanwhile, of course answer it. But letting the woods "settle down" for a few minutes after your entry is a good idea. If you get a reply after your first call, answer. If not, wait at least a full minute. Follow this spacing for perhaps three series. If there is still no reply, wait five or ten minutes. Whatever sort of reply you get, make your reply in kind, that is, gentle, or strident and challenging. After twenty or thirty minutes, it's probably time to move. But be sure you remain ever alert, for as I have stated quite often a squirrel may come in without a sound or be moving around looking for you.

Calling in spring and summer, where there are open seasons or just for fun, is often very successful because you are dealing with a good many young, naive animals. Early in the fall season, calling is just as successful. But as hunting season continues, any area where pressure is severe is certain to have many "wised-up" squirrels. Calling with angry sounds may make the squirrels wary. It may indicate to them that a squirrel has become suspicious. But soft calling with a different rhythm will sound contented and placating.

Make this a series of quiet barks. Cup one hand around the open end of the barrel, and strike the bellows against the other palm, cupping this other palm also to soften the sound. The call goes like this: *Chuck, chuck, chuck, chuck, chuck.* Pause, then repeat. The series is not as swift as the aroused call I described earlier. Squirrels make sounds other than those given here, such as the harsh, complaining and angry long-drawn *Kuaa-a-a-a!* uttered by grays that often precedes a series of yakking barks. But the simple sounds noted are all you need to imitate.

Youngsters learn a lot as they practice talking to squirrels

In several of the Rocky Mountain states — Colorado, New Mexico, Arizona — are found the tufted-eared Abert squirrels. These big, strikingly handsome animals dwell in the forests of immense yellow pine, and indeed seem "tied" to them, feeding on buds and seeds. During open seasons I have hunted them and found the sport most interesting and unique. I have never known of anyone calling them. Yet it certainly could be done. Although they are quiet much of the time, they are likely to erupt over some small annoyance into a tirade of scolding and chattering. Their bark is rather similar to that of large fox squirrels. A relative, fully protected, is the Kaibab squirrel found only on the Kaibab Plateau on the north rim of the Grand Canyon. I suspect that calling might be a successful way of bringing this squirrel near enough for photographs.

Whether you are an avid squirrel hunter, or a person who simply likes to watch these agile, interesting animals, you will find that a call will enhance both opportunity and success and create enjoyable moments. Squirrel calling is also an endeavor for practically every outdoors-minded person, for the range of the several species takes in the major share of the United States.

12

Predators

IN THE WORLD of animal calling some of the most dramatic experiences of all are to be had with the predators. Into this category fall all of the meat eaters. Most plentiful of these are the foxes—red and gray—and the coyote. Next is the bobcat. The large predators—mountain lion, bears, jaguar—are also occasionally responsive. And among the smaller animals in this group, the raccoon, badger, ringtail cat, and even skunk and opossum will come to a call. Meat eating birds such as hawks and owls can also be called.

The basis of all predator calling is an appeal to the animal's instinct to kill and eat some other animal or bird. The predator may not actually be very hungry. But in the lives of all creatures both feast and famine are ever present. Therefore, they seize any opportunity for an easy meal. Although the diets of all predators are mixed to some extent—fresh meat, carrion, berries, nuts, vegetation—fresh-killed meat is usually preferred. Yet fresh meat is the most difficult to obtain and requires the greatest expenditure of physical effort. However, practically over the entire continent, wherever predators roam, one small forage animal is usually abundant, universally known to and sought by the meat eaters. This is the rabbit, one of the easiest meals for alert predators to catch.

Whenever a predator catches a rabbit, this otherwise non-vocal animal screams in fright and pain. It will do the same if it happens to get caught somehow, in a thornbush, under a fence, by a snake, or when it is accidentally injured. Predators know this sound, having heard it and undoubtedly responded to it often, to pick off an easy meal or to share one, or to battle over one with another predator. It is the fairly simple imitation of this squall of a rabbit in its death throes upon which all predator calling is based.

There are some variations. Rodents such as mice are also diet staples for predators. Long ago Indians knew how to "squeak up" foxes. Many a pioneer hunter and trapper learned that trick, too. Modern call makers offer "short-range" rodent-squeak calls. They have also concocted recordings of such sounds as trapped woodpeckers, meadow larks and other birds chattering in distress. These, too, bring predators in. Taped sounds of the quavering bleats of goat kids also have been effective, in areas where many goats are raised and foxes, coyotes and bobcats prey upon them. The recorded squealing and barking of baby foxes is occasionally used to call adult foxes. However, because anguished rabbit sounds are loud, thus carrying very well over long range, and are so well recognized by all predators, these are the sounds most used. They are effective everywhere.

A scattering of old-time outdoorsmen knew about this phenomenon years ago, but it is only over the past couple of decades that predator calls have been available, and that the sport of predator calling has grown so fantastically in popularity. Once one has experienced the high drama of a first successful calling session, he instantly realizes why interest in this endeavor has boomed. I vividly remember some of my early experiences and how absolutely amazed I was.

Murry Burnham here talks a coyote in almost close enough to touch.

There was the time, for example, when the Burnham brothers and I made a trip down into eastern Mexico and camped on a large ranch along the coast not far from the village of San Fernando. Coyotes and bobcats were swarming in this wild country, and the ranch owner was happy to have us experimenting with calls in the hope that we'd thin down the predator population. Needless to say, no predator call had ever been blown in this region. The predator population was dense enough to cause plenty of competition for food, and the animals therefore were not the least bit skittish. Nothing had ever bothered them.

At one place we stopped our Jeep in mesquite shade along a ranch trail, got out and sat against it, one of us on either side, one in front. Thus we could watch in all directions. The day was still — midday — not the best time for calling because predators lie up and rest in cover as a rule throughout these hours. Winston did the calling, sitting in front, in the middle of the trail. Instantly a big coyote bounded out of the brush possibly three hundred yards down the trail and came as fast as it could run.

Before it reached us, two more were coming on my side, and I learned later that another pair were running at Murry on the far side. We were all in camouflage clothing and in shade. The Jeep didn't seem to inhibit these animals at all. They simply swarmed, racing around us in a wild melee, hackles up and eyes blazing. We were all so mesmerized nobody shot. The animals circled within a few yards and ran off, looking finally as astonished as we did. Afterward Winston continued calling, and before we quit the spot we had brought in eleven coyotes!

To one for the first time seeing a predator come rushing to a call, the experience is just about unbelievable. It is a kind of magic. Because predator calling has become so popular and is practiced far and wide, in most places nowadays a substantial amount of finesse is required. Animals have become wary. Foxes and coyotes fooled once, whether shot at and missed or only photographed, become difficult to call. Youngsters raised by a mother that has been taken in a couple of times undoubtedly have some of the caution passed down to them.

Nonetheless, predator calling still gets astonishing results. It is an extremely effective way of getting unusual close-up photos. With fur prices high it is also utilized by trappers as an easier means to the same end. Where a particular predator or group of them have become nuisances, preying on livestock, calling can be a most selective manner of eliminating the problem animals. When the sport was first getting started some few years ago there was a lot of indiscriminate shooting of the called animals, for no very logical reasons. There is not much of that nowadays. A few trophies are taken, and where needed, predator populations are controlled. But hundreds of callers currently work on predators just for the fun of bringing them in.

Cats come to call in various ways. A bobcat, above, may do anything from charging to sitting at some distance. Left, this Mexican jaguar first sought vantage from above. Stalking an anguished amplifier, below, this mountain lion provided the author one of his greatest calling thrills.

HOW TO CALL

A large number of mouth-blown calls are now available. Among them they differ a good deal in tone, depending on the type of reed used and how they are tuned. Most expert callers prefer a fairly coarse scream. To work properly a call should give a range of several notes as more breath is applied. The majority of predator calls are pitched to imitate the screams of an injured cottontail. However, lower pitched calls are also available to mimic more closely the cry of a jack rabbit or a snowshoe hare. Either will work, but it is best to use one matching the rabbits most abundant in the area. The best practice in some areas is to use two, and settle on the one that gets the most consistent results.

A close-range predator call, like this one by Olt, leaves the caller's hands free to operate either a gun or camera.

    The basic sound upon which the calling series are based may be spelled *waaaaaaa*. You cup your hand, almost closed, around the end of the call, and as you blow, open your hand. At the same time push your breath through harder. Thus the effect is about like this: *waaaaaAAAA*. Almost all makers of predator calls also offer instruction records. It is a good idea to listen to some of these, especially those that were made by well-known and truly expert callers. Trying to imitate as precisely as you can the recorded sounds will speed up your learning process. There are even actual recordings of screams of predator-caught rabbits, and of course these "say it" in a most authentic manner.

    Try to visualize what happens, for example, when a hawk swoops down and seizes a cottontail. It is a cruel business, but that's the way nature

operates. As the talons hit home the rabbit utters a scream of pain and terror. This is repeated in several syllables. They are not run together but are
distinctly separated—*waaaaAAA, waaaaAAA, waaaaAAA*. This first multiple scream is loud. But now the sound continues in shorter squalls, urgent
and anguished. To imitate this, you open your hand each time from
around the end of the call. But these shorter syllables are done with uneven
breath to get a quavering effect. Volume diminishes; the rabbit is mortally
hurt and weakening. *WaaaaAA- waaaaA-waaaaA- waaa.*

Individual callers work out techniques and series that seem to get the
best results for them generally, or in a certain area. Usually it is best to
begin with the wild, loud squalls, follow with the quavering, diminishing
routine, and even add a few short, weak cries: *waaaa-waaaa-waaa-waaa.*
After this you should pause at least thirty seconds. Now give another series,
but delete the introductory loud scream. From here on repeat this series
every forty-five to sixty seconds. You can intermingle this with a few
muffled, wavering, weak cries.

It may be that you will see your quarry almost instantly after the first
series of calls. If so, and if it is coming swiftly, don't call again. Let the
animal come. If it starts to circle and trot away, then try to coax it back by
low, plaintive quavering calls, but not too loud. Too much unnatural volume will arouse suspicion. If nothing shows after fifteen or twenty minutes,
you just may be working a "dry run." But never be in a rush to leave.
Sometimes sticking it out for half an hour brings an animal such as a coyote
from literally a mile away. Or, the constant calling whets the curiosity of a
wary fox or coyote and it finally decides to have a look.

Of the three predators most commonly called—foxes, coyotes, bobcats—
the coyote will usually come the farthest simply because it is a strong, wide-
ranging, swift animal. Bobcats come slowly as a rule. I've seen one fiddle
around for half an hour, sneaking from bush to bush. At any rate, it's a
good idea to make a second stand at least a mile, perhaps farther, from the
first one. Although you can call too much when working on coyotes, which
are very suspicious and sharp, steady calling is very effective on both foxes
and bobcats. Coyotes and red foxes rather often race straight toward the
caller even across open terrain. Bobcats and gray foxes are more insistent
on moving in cover.

However, one of the most intriguing facets of predator calling is that
every individual animal seems to react in a different way. Once while calling
in a gully in desert country, I happened to look carefully around and to my
amazement saw a big bobcat sitting calmly on the bank about thirty yards
away, staring at me. On another occasion Winston Burnham and I were
hidden in brush, just off a ranch trail, calling for coyotes. We could hear
behind us the sound of a big coyote coming all-out at us. Its feet were hit-
ting the hard dirt audibly. It sounded louder, louder and I finally jumped
up. The animal had been intent on Winston's position, some yards ahead of

This running coyote came expecting an easy meal, caught the author's scent, and here is about to turn inside-out in an effort to get away.

me. It almost brushed my leg as it hurtled past, snarling at me because it was so startled.

The next one we called on that same day came stealing in silently. We had not seen any movement anywhere—and then suddenly there it was, facing us through brush a short distance away. If they do not get the wind on you, and you are well camouflaged and hidden, both foxes and coyotes will occasionally stand some yards away and growl or bark, suspicious but puzzled. Windy days are poor calling days because the animals can't hear as well and are always more nervous. They will also circle to get the wind on the caller's location. Sometimes a bobcat will pay no attention to the wind or to man scent. A coyote will leave instantly when it picks up scent or any motion.

The gray fox, plentiful across the South, responds readily. The fox may occasionally climb a stub to look down upon the source of the noise.

A prime rule of predator calling is always to call into the wind, and to watch the 180-degree arc in that direction. If there are two hunters or callers working together, a good plan is to sit back to back so each can watch his own arc for possible activity. Some callers hide in a thicket and call standing up. It's better to sit down. Sit against something, not behind it. Hunching up in the shade of a bush and wearing full camouflage is a good plan. You should also sit so that you can see well over a broad expanse, but of course never sit atop a ridge where you are easily spotted.

Although predator calling is a year-round activity, late summer, or through the fall and well into winter are the months likely to produce the most outstanding results. There are good reasons for this. In spring and early summer there is generally an abundance of food. By late summer some food sources are tapering off, and in addition young predators are now out of the dens and on their own, and they are rather naive. As fall progresses and changes to winter, the younger animals mature and wise up, but food availability diminishes, and so competition for it becomes more severe.

The best times of day are the dawn and early morning hours, and the late afternoon up until dark. All predators also move and hunt at night. We will discuss night calling for them a little later. However, in quite a few places night calling has been made illegal, and in others it is illegal to be calling at night and carrying a gun. This is to help eliminate deer poachers who use predator calling as an excuse. Some members of the calling fraternity also frown on night calling, considering it a harmful influence to the sport. Frankly, I don't feel that way about it at all. Predator calling at night is an extremely exciting business. You don't even need to carry a gun or do any shooting. It is great for flash photos, and there are other aspects of it — which I'll shortly cover — that are extremely intriguing.

Further, some animals that will seldom respond to a call in the daytime are easily called at night. Raccoons and ringtails are the prime examples. I've spent some interesting evenings calling and photographing ringtails, which are plentiful in the Texas Hill Country where I live. The fur is also valuable and many a ranch youngster has learned how to collect twenty dollars or more a night with his predator call, a scoped .22 and a light. The Burnhams used to do a little trick for visitors who had never experienced predator calling, by going out at night carrying a long-handled net, and coaxing raccoons so close they could scoop them up.

As I've stated, the middle of the day is not the best period for calling, and especially so if the weather is hot. On cool, overcast days, or in winter when the animal is forage hunting, responses may be had all day long. On days of high wind, however, there is little sense in calling. Further, when you are calling coyotes and — as I mentioned earlier — they start to bark and howl the moment you blow your call, you may about as well forget it. They've been alerted to your presence and aren't going to have anything to do with you. I also want to note here that predator calling in snow country where winters are severe is extremely effective. This is a difficult time for the animals to find food, and their caution sometimes diminishes in direct proportion. Obviously the caller should wear white.

MECHANICAL DEVICES

Before we go further, perhaps this is a good place to look at the matter of mechanical calls. These have been very popular over the past few years, and have been highly improved from what the originals were. In some ways they are more awkward to use than simply blowing a call. But there are also advantages, such as authenticity of sounds, no errors, and the ease with which the caller can operate.

Tape recorder-players like this one have many uses such as playing instructional tapes, playing "endless" calling tapes in the wilds, recording for playback your practice sessions, and recording the calls of live animals. When used to call animals, the speaker unit can be placed 25 to 50 feet away to lessen the chance that you'll be detected.

There are several types of these calls. The first ones were simply record players that ran on batteries. These, now much refined, are still very popular and effective. Most of these use a speaker with a twenty-five or fifty foot cord. It is hung in a bush, or set on the ground well out away from the hiding place of the caller. If there is any breeze, the speaker is pointed into it. If the day is calm, most callers point the speaker up so sound is evenly disseminated. Often a piece of camo net is draped over the speaker.

The hidden caller plugs in the speaker cord, sets the player level, starts it and gets the needle tracking, with the volume turned down to eliminate record noise. Once the recorded calling or actual recorded rabbit sounds begin, the volume is turned up. Intervals between call series are either on the record, or else are accomplished by turning the volume clear down.

When an animal is seen and is coming in, the volume is also turned down, or the machine turned off. It is amusing sometimes to watch an animal come right up to the place where the speaker is and puzzle over it. I shot a photo one time of a big lion that slunk right up to the speaker, which was not hidden, and spit at it!

The next step in manufacture of mechanical calls came with the advent of popularly-priced tape players that ran on batteries, and in which tape cassettes could be used. Some of these today look similar to the record players, speaker and all, except that they accept tapes. Others are more compact and need no speaker or cord. The use of "endless" tapes eliminates any need to turn a record over or start it over. Variations of volume are handled in the same way. Some of the smaller, refined units are easy to conceal and to use, and they are not as bulky to carry as the larger players with speakers.

These mechanical calls, which sell anywhere in the range from $50 to $60 to upwards of $200, are without question most effective. They also eliminate the need for a caller's having to learn to do his own imitations. For those who will call only occasionally, the mechanical callers are a good idea. And of course they can be used for virtually any kind of calling, if you buy the records or tapes, from moose to squirrels as well as predators. And you also can play "how-to" tapes and records. Note well that they are not legal for waterfowl hunting. They proved so effective they were long ago outlawed.

MOUTH-BLOWN CALLS

The simple mouth-blown call, however, is a whole lot less bother to carry and operate, much less expensive, and it can be better matched to the whims and reactions of individual predators, and callers. A recorded moose call needs to say only one thing. An expert predator caller may need to coax and cajole animals, and the simple turning up or down of volume is not always the answer. Let me give you a classic example.

A good many call makers offer what are known as standard "long range" predator calls, with matching "short range" ones. The latter are usually some kind of small, low-volume "squeaker." Sometimes a fox or cat or coyote will come just so far and no farther. Yet it may not appear frightened. It is simply uncertain. If you try to use a regular rabbit squall now, with the animal at close range and fully attentive right on your hiding spot, you have to be awfully good at calling to get results. But a very quiet, low-volume mouse squeak may so puzzle and arouse the animal—after it has come all this way to a squalling rabbit—that it cannot resist coming further. I have on many occasions watched the Burnhams play this trick. They make a short-range squeaker, but when calling they often imitate a mouse squeak by sucking with lips pressed against the back of a hand, or the palm,

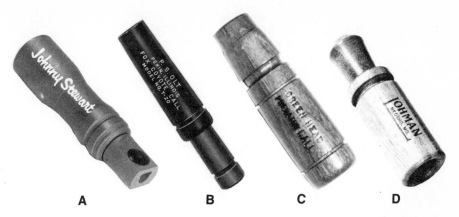

Predator calls. (A) This Johnny Stewart piece emits long- and short-range rabbit sounds, which can be controlled by teeth and lips. Olt **(B)** and Green Head **(C)** calls also imitate the ubiquitous rabbit. The Lohman Coon Talker **(D)** produces a low-pitched growl that arouses a coon's curiosity.

Small "squeakers" produce the sounds of rodents and work well at close-range.

or between two close-held fingers. They have learned to do this expertly. One time Winston, covered with a net and lying down, had a gray fox leap right on him when he tricked it this way!

There are also many variations that can be tried with a mouth blown call. Blowing through one and trilling with your tongue back of your teeth — like a running-motor sound — will produce a chattering sound almost identical to the noises made by birds such as woodpeckers trapped or in trouble. At times this is extremely effective on raccoons and foxes. Also, a good caller can muffle his call, hunch over and emit short, quavering wails of low volume that almost plead with a predator to come in and finish off this poor, suffering cottontail. Thus, for the hobbyist who is willing to put in some time learning to use a predator call to its fullest advantage, the mouth-blown call is not restricted to set routines as are the mechanical recordings.

Carrying this thinking a step farther, a good many callers have found that in their area a certain call, pitched just so, gets better results than several others. Why this should be is not clear, but it happens. Also, in a given area a caller fiddles with calling routines, and suddenly hits one that really brings 'em in almost every time. Maybe this is unorthodox, but he should stick to it, because for him, in that place, it works. The mouth-blown call allows all sorts of latitude. One can "make it up as he goes along."

It occurs to me as I write this that most calling instructions — even those I gave a few pages back — state that you should launch the calling from any given stand by letting fly with a loud scream of anguish. I know a caller who operates on the plains in South Dakota who never varies this routine. He goes on the assumption that no matter how carefully he gets into position, any animals close to him that might be frightened by the unnaturally loud rabbit scream, will already have sneaked away. His loud beginning gets the attention of distant animals. He is extremely successful, and often picks up in his binocular — *a must item of equipment for predator callers* — coyotes or foxes coming on the lope boldly and at hundreds of yards distant.

Now here is the other side. Another friend does his calling, for coyotes and bobcats, in an expanse of dense prickly pear cactus and thornbrush in southern Texas not far from the Mexican border. He silently sneaks into the cover and to the edge of some small opening. He begins with a mouse squeak. There are pack rat nests galore in the pear clumps and these abundant animals are common diet for the predators. You never know, in such cover, where an animal may have bedded down. It can be anywhere, whereas on the plains specific spots such as draws or small headers would be the obvious places.

I was with this friend one day when we left the vehicle and walked soundlessly up a *sendero*, or trail, eased into a stand of tall pear, threaded through part of it and hunkered at the edge of an opening not over twenty feet in diameter. This was right in the middle of the day. He squeaked three times—and a big coyote literally catapulted into the opening. Obviously it had been lying down just across in the cover on the other side. Had he sounded off with a loud rabbit scream we'd never have known the animal was there. Thus, this man's technique in heavy cover is always to start quietly, even if you use the rabbit sound. This avoids frightening nearby animals. After you have established whether or not any are nearby, there is ample time to speak to the distances.

OTHER ESSENTIALS

It is certainly more enjoyable for two or more callers to work together. Now and then having a partner can be advantageous, for example, in watching a wide expanse of terrain. Some callers believe that, in country where bobcats are plentiful, two callers sitting a few yards apart and calling, can bring cats in much better than a single caller. Incidentally, bobcats are extremely secretive creatures. They are more plentiful, even sometimes right around towns and cities, than is generally believed. They are very susceptible to calling but not predictable. At any rate, though it may be more fun with two or more hunters together, a lone operator is more likely to get the heavy action. There is less chance of noise and of movement, and there is less scent spreading from the stand.

When I was first learning, with some expert help, to call coyotes and foxes, it was common practice to drive across a ranch, just stop the car anywhere, get out and stand beside the vehicle to call. Sometimes two or three coyotes would bound out and run right at the car. Today predators are far more sophisticated. For consistent success, you must get to your stand as unobtrusively as possible. Leave your vehicle hidden behind a hill, in a gully, or around a bend in the trail. Don't slam doors or talk. Get well away from the vehicle, moving either into or across the wind.

If you are in rolling country, walk up a slope, crawl over the top, and when you are well below the crest, sit in shadow of bushes, or against a rock or big tree trunk. A vantage point like this on a ridge side, in "fresh" territory gives you every break and allows you to scrutinize a wide sweep of terrain. Always wear camouflage clothing. It's a good idea to extend this to include headnet and gloves. To be sure, many callers simply wear drab clothing and sit against something to break up outlines. That will do, but full camo will do better over the long haul. Never make any quick moves. Be very deliberate if you must move at all, and in raising or lowering the call. Be sure to sit so that you don't have to peer around trees or bushes to see properly.

Don't be in any great hurry to start calling. Get properly settled, size up the country within your view. There are always spots that seem most likely for animals to be hiding in, or hunting in—a brushy gully, a jumbled outcrop of rocks, a patch or strip of cover on a plain, brushy cover around a waterhole, a natural runway in a draw. Fence rows grown to weeds, the intersections of trails, and ranch roads that have brush or woods along them are excellent places to watch. Size it all up for several minutes and then begin calling. That way you aren't so likely to be taken by surprise.

If a fox, cat or coyote is seen, you can judge from its reactions what you should do. Don't coax it unless it needs coaxing. If it hesitates, let it know where you are. But always cut the volume down in proportion to the distance of the animal. The closer it comes—in case you have to plead with it—the lower the volume should be. Small, weak cries, as if the "rabbit" is about to give up the ghost, are often irresistible. If you are in territory where both foxes and coyotes range, you may find the foxes a bit timid. They are skittish of tangling with their larger relatives. But where only foxes live they often come racing to the call.

In any region where there are trails, of any kind, always watch them closely, even as you travel. Foxes and coyotes commonly travel them and of course leave droppings along them. Bobcats are more inclined to follow draws and gullies and stream courses. Look for their tracks. Often abundant sign will point you to prime calling territory. Raccoons will gorge on such items as wild black or choke cherries and leave droppings everywhere beneath such trees. Ringtail cats of the southwest invariably leave their scats atop a rock. By noting these, you can easily gauge the ringtail population.

In an earlier chapter I discussed scents. Mask scents such as skunk are a help in regions where predators are extra shy. Urine scents have some attraction value. Mask scents such as rabbit scent wiped on boots and boot soles undoubtedly are a help when you must walk to a stand and possibly cross territory an incoming animal may cross. I've watched coyotes whirl and flee instantly when they came to a fresh man track.

LARGE PREDATORS

As noted, coyotes, bobcats and foxes are the mainstays of the predator calling sport. The chances of calling the larger animals, and even the opportunities to try, are very limited. Mountain lions have been called on a number of occasions. In Mexico one time, calling at night, the Burnhams and I had one come in behind us. We were about to move, Winston turned on the big light and swept it around. Needless to say, we got a bit of a start when it came to rest on a big lion crouched fifty or sixty yards away.

The problems in lion calling, however, are many. For one thing, the chief diet of lions is made up of deer and, within proper range, javelina. Thus they are not very predictable. A dying rabbit won't necessarily intrigue any lion that hears the sound. But the exciting other side is that it may. A scattering of callers have brought lions in, and a few lions have been taken that way as trophies. The toughest part of lion calling is getting to where you have a fair chance that one will hear your call. As everyone knows, lions are uncommon, and on any given range are not likely to be numerous, even though not endangered. Consensus among those who have been successful at calling them seems to be that one must operate in known lion country, range out widely in it, be willing to stay on a stand calling hard for at least half an hour and perhaps an hour. When a lion does come to a call, it usually comes in with great stealth, in typical cat fashion. It is suddenly there and the caller is wondering how it got there. At the very least this is an exciting challenge, although successful results are rare.

The same is true of black bears. A fair number have been called. They may take a long time coming in, but may come in a headlong rush when they do make up their mind. Some others will pass distantly, pausing to look and test the wind, but keep right on going. Results are by no means predictable. Further, it is difficult to get into an area where bears are abundant enough so there's a fair chance that one will hear the call. Those who have been successful have operated invariably in places thick with bear sign, and called long and loud. It may well be that black bear calling would be known as more successful an endeavor if more people gave it a serious try.

The expert, long-experienced Burnhams have had some modest success on jaguars, and they found ocelots and margay cats in Mexico easy to call. In the past, jaguar calling has always been accomplished by imitating the roar of another jaguar. But this was chiefly to locate animals so that hounds might be put on them.

SMALL PREDATORS

Among the smaller animals raccoons and ringtails are responsive at night. Raccoons can be called by using a regular injured rabbit call, but callers have paid some special attention to raccoons. Raccoons habitually feed along lake shores, stream courses, and saltwater marshes. Hunting at night they are often able to catch water oriented birds. They know well the sounds made by distressed or disturbed birds such as sea gulls, shore birds and others. Calls are made – Herter's has one – to imitate these sounds. To the prowling raccoons, the sound need not be a specific bird, but the call lures raccoons if it sounds like a bird in trouble.

To avoid confusion, callers should know that certain calls advertised for raccoons have a quite different and specialized purpose. One, for example, made by Green Head, is called a "Coon Talker." Its sound imitates the hoarse squall of a raccoon in difficulty, as when dogs have grabbed it. It is not for calling raccoons to you, but is used, instead, by hound hunters after they have treed a raccoon. It causes the animal to look down so its eyes can be shined, and when raucously blown along with the beating of brush and dog sounds, it often causes the treed animal to jump.

Predator calls turn up a great variety of animals. Here a normally nocturnal badger responds. His chief fare is rodents.

Badgers are most efficient killers of small animals and birds, and will readily respond to a call. But they are nowhere particularly abundant. Nor are they built for swift long-distance races. On the plains, badgers are incidentals almost always, a bonus for the caller who is after coyotes, foxes or bobcats. Big owls sometimes come whooshing in at night to perch near a caller. Hawks often have a look at a spot from which the anguished rabbit sound emanates. Once I sat on a slope just below its crest wearing a gray wool cap and blowing a call for coyotes. A hawk sailed over the ridgetop, barely skimming it, saw the cap, and I caught the flicker of movement out the edge of my eye just in time to yell and duck.

It is interesting indeed that all of the animal and bird predators respond so positively to their own hunger pangs and instinct that they are quick to take advantage of an easy kill. And it is a wry compliment of sorts to rabbits and rodents that they have been such successful colonizers that their squalls of pain and their squeaks are instantly recognized everywhere by all meat eaters as an opportunity. Because most of the predaceous species are active at night as well as by day, much of the early modern history of this endeavor was experienced after dark. Much of my own beginning experiences in fact occurred then.

CALLING AT NIGHT

Calling after dark requires two kinds of lights. One is the headlamp, the other is a big long-range, bright-beam light used only to pinpoint an animal for shooting. Some of the big lights are flashlights, and some are made with long cord and handle to plug into cigar lighters in vehicles. I well recall some of the early dramatic results of calling at night about fifteen years ago with the Burnhams. The one who was to do the calling was the only man who had his headlamp turned on, and who carried the big flashlight.

We left the vehicle quietly, walked silently single file some distance away to a spot we'd selected during the day. Moonless nights are by far the best nights for calling. Bright moonlight allows the animals to see your movements too easily. Our use of the headlamp followed strict routine. While walking to the spot, if we used the lamp at all, we cast its beam onto the ground close ahead of the first man. Sometimes we felt our way along a trail in total darkness.

Once at the calling spot, we switched the headlamp on but turned its beam upward. In other words, the beam did not touch the ground. In addition, we always tried to get headlamps with dimmer switches on them so that the light could be turned down just as low as possible. The idea of the headlamp was *not* to pick up incoming animals in its beam. In fact, the direct beam is frightening to coyotes and foxes, and sometimes to cats also. But when the beam is pointed upward or straight out into the air, the wide angle of the lamp lays a broad but weak glow in a half circle in front of the caller. The eyes of incoming animals glow in it. The animal may not be visible at all.

The procedure, as we followed it, was that the shooters — if we were intending to do any shooting — stood back to back with the caller, and turned just enough so that they could watch the arc of the glow of light on the ground, too. The caller, as he blew the call, slowly swung his head from side to side. Thus the glowing arc covered a full 180 degrees or more in steady sweeps. Because of the angle of the light just above his eyes, the caller often picked up the glow of an eye while the shooter or shooters did not see it. So, we watched closely what he did. If his head ceased swinging, we knew he had something coming in. Much of the excitement, in areas where coyotes, foxes and cats all roamed was that you never knew what might be coming.

If the caller raised his hand and began squeaking softly, we knew he was coaxing something in closer. If he quit and began louder calling and swinging the light again, we knew whatever had been there had gone. The highest drama came when his head stopped, the calling stopped or turned to low squeaking, ad the other hand holding the big light came up. When the light stabbed into the blackness to outline some predator, things happened fast. A coyote would not stand long in the light. A fox might stand

Night calling produces some surprises. Here an owl alights just one perch short of the fortunate caller's head.

momentarily. A bobcat might do anything — run, sit down, walk right at us — we never could predict.

We made a good many night calling jaunts without doing any shooting. We were just learning and observing. Later the Burnhams devised a light that could be mounted on a gun so that it would not shine into the scope. It utilized a mercury switch. As long as the gun is held on its side, the light is off. Bring it to shooting position, and the light is instantly switched on and pointed right on the target.

Several years ago, an invention came along, borrowed from its original use in some zoos, that has revolutionized the night calling of predators. This is the red headlamp and red spotlight. The basis for its use is an amazing slice of nature lore.

The animal predators, and some other animals also, such as deer, lack the cells in their eyes that can distinguish colors. Therefore they are color blind, and live in a world of gray shades. That is, they see all light or color as all the intermediate shadings and intensities from black to white. A white light such as the headlamp and the bright spotlight are seen just as they are—white lights can be blinding, or at the very least frightening.

Some few years ago managers of several zoos pondered how to exhibit nocturnal animals. These animals retreated to their sleeping quarters by day and were active at night. But they were frightened and retreated again if lights were used. So, experiments were done with light of varying colors. It was soon evident that a rich red light had practically no effect on the animals. They could be seen in it, but they did not seem to realize it was there. They reacted this way because to them the light was not red, but a subdued gray. So the effect was about the same as having no light present, or at most a very weak, hazy one.

Finally the idea was carried over to predator calling at night. The Burnhams were among the first in this interesting field. During the testing stages we made a trip together, and I did an article on it for one of the national magazines—the first written on the subject. Also we made some of the first photos of night calling's phenomenal effects ever taken in the world. Some photos were taken at full dusk and some after dark, using no flash but simply the available red light. During these experiments a big bobcat stood and stared at us, having come to the call, with the big red spotlight fully on it. The cat seemed unable to notice that any light was present.

This red light was a tremendous advance, for it meant there was no need to avoid throwing a beam on incoming animals. In fact, tests have proved that if human scent and sound are avoided, predators will come right into a circle of red light from a big flood or spotlight. What this discovery means for the hunter is obvious. But it is also even more important for the wildlife

For night calling this Convertible Light by Burnham Brothers shoots either a concentrated red beam or a long-reach white beam. The 15-foot cord plugs into an auto cigarette lighter or an adapter that connects to a 12-volt battery.

This is the scope-mounted light, turned on by a mercury switch when the rifle comes into shooting position.

observers and hobbyists, and for photographers. Further—and aside from calling—some persons have pursued the red light matter further, and have put up feeders in their yards with red lights flooding them, in order to attract such nocturnal animals as raccoons, opossums, and ringtails.

Again I must emphasize that night calling, even when you are not hunting, is illegal in some states. So be certain how the laws affect your activities. However, in locations where you may use a light and a call but not a gun, I can assure you the fun and excitement of night predator calling is indeed intriguing.

POINTS TO PONDER

Daytime predator calling, whether just for the enjoyment of "watching 'em run at you," or else armed only with a movie or still camera, is a dramatic hobby in its own right. You do not need to be way back in the wilderness, either. Foxes live on the fringes of towns and cities, and throughout the entire west and in some midwestern and eastern states, too, coyotes are found not very far outside the cities. Bobcats are more difficult to find, and sometimes more difficult to call, too. But they do not necessarily live only in remote areas.

Another point to emphasize is that predator calling may sound difficult simply because we're dealing with crafty creatures. But the fact is, it is fundamentally one of the simplest and easiest of all calling categories. You really need to learn only one basic sound, and then use it in varying volumes, pitches and series. That's all. As long as you get into your calling country without being detected, remain quiet and immobile and well hidden, and always keep the wind in your favor, there are few errors you can

Wearing a headlamp with red beam that is invisible to predators, the caller holds a young coyote close until the camera flash provides startling illumination.

possibly make. On young animals of the year especially — such as foxes and coyotes in early fall — even a first-timer can be successful.

What should you consider as "being successful?" Certainly you won't call up an animal every time you try. In terrain where the quarry is moderately abundant, you might expect to see the "magic" once every five to ten stands you make. But there may also be long spells of dry runs, when out of twenty or thirty stands you will draw all blanks. Then one day, in a particular spot, every stand you make will have an animal all but running over you. Perseverance and patience are the watch words.

Be sure to follow the simple instructions I've given. Separate each wail or *waaaaa* distinctly in the series, almost as if you are saying into the call: *tu-WAA, tu-WAA, tu-WAA, tu-WAA.* Then when you taper off in volume, make it quaver. The urgency, the fright, the pain, the terror — imagine what the poor rabbit is going through, growing weaker and slowly dying. That's really all there is to it — and the first time you see a coyote or fox or cat coming at you, you probably will feel as I felt: You won't be able to believe it. And from there on you'll never be able to quit!

13

Refinements and the Future

IN THE FIRST CHAPTER of this book I stated that there is probably no creature on earth wholly unresponsive to calling. Trouble is, even though a great deal is already known about game calling there is still much to be discovered. A good many years ago I developed an intense interest in the so-called shore birds. This large group includes snipe, avocet, stilts, curlews, godwits, willets, and many other modest-sized birds of beach and shore. During early years of settlement in this country the shorebirds were prime targets for gunners. They are all delicious eating.

Much market hunting was done for them, and because they were not very prolific, they did not survive the pressure. All hunting of them was stopped very early in this century. The only member of the group presently hunted is the jacksnipe. A very old gentleman I knew long ago in Pennsylvania had been an ardent shorebird hunter during the 1800s. I was greatly intrigued with his tales of decoying flocks of shorebirds, and of imitating some of their cries. Later I made decoys for jacksnipe and used them successfully.

During some winters spent in Florida in the 1940s, I was able to observe thousands of shorebirds along the saltwater beaches of the keys. Willets were favorites because of their most musical call—*will-willet, will-willet*. I got so I could whistle a fairly authentic imitation and easily got birds to answer. On several occasions I have photographed long-billed curlews and listened to their mellow, musical skirling *cur-loooo*. And this, too, I have been able to mimic well enough to produce replies.

In eastern Mexico on one trip I hunted a number of different game birds, among them the noisy chachalaca, a drab-colored bird related distantly to the pheasants and "gallinaceous," or chicken-like, birds. The raucous, incessant calls of the chachalaca almost exactly speak the name. Fiddling with a predator call, I was able to produce a series of syllables — *cha-cha-la-ca-cha-cha-la-ca* — that invariably elicited replies.

Thus I would urge readers who become intrigued with the hobby of bird and animal calling to take every opportunity to enlarge its boundaries. I remember, as I write, stopping in a restaurant years ago in Gallup, New Mexico, where a mocking bird, raised from a youngster, was kept in a cage. We spent half an hour trying to stump the bird, whistling fragments and listening for its copy. It was almost "un-stump-able." Outside my office door here in the Texas countryside mocking birds are always carrying on. I can get them to repeat whistled phrases.

The fact is, a vast area of calling could be uncovered if song bird watchers would show more ingenuity in actively attempting to bring the birds to them. It is surprising that so very little has been learned or even attempted in this field, what with the large organizations interested in song birds. The birds' songs, their mating calls and alarm cries, and their simple

Shorebirds are responsive to carefully-intoned renditions of their calls. This long-billed curlew replies to facsimiles of his liquid *cur-looo*.

songs of contentment are well known, yet practically no serious experiments are made to imitate them or to find out which sounds they will respond to.

Some groups of non-game birds are easily called. Various owls are readily susceptible during mating season. Their cat-like squalls and coarse squawks, imitated by mouth by the few who know how, charm them literally right out of the trees. The "Turkey Hooter" call mentioned in Chapter 5 simulates the hoot of a great horned owl. It is easy to arouse owls to answer this call, thus giving away their positions. Hawks are of course even more easily called, and a number of call makers offer hawk calls. These are used, as we've seen, to frighten pheasants or quail, to arouse crows, but they can also bring flying hawks near for a look.

Several years ago I was goose hunting in the rice country outside Houston, Texas with Lyle Jordan, my guide, who does a perfect imitation of the *screeee* call of a circling hawk. We hunched among our large spread, dressed in white parkas so we'd match the white of the snow goose decoys. A hawk was circling the field, which is common. The birds watched for crippled ducks and geese and pounced upon them. Lyle called to the hawk. It circled several times, and finally dropped low. The bird called softly, and Jordan kept replying. We had it over us, within a few feet.

ADVANCES AND EXPERIMENTS IN CALLING

I would predict that there will be much scientific experimentation in the next few years in a number of unusual categories, in an attempt to learn the languages of many kinds of life. In the opening chapter I mentioned experimental recordings made of fish sounds. For a long time scents have been used in sport fishing, to attract various species to a bait or lure. Some modern lures have a built-in scent that oozes when the lure is wet. It is allegedly attractive to certain game fish. Other lures nowadays use small air chambers with a rattle inside. As the lure vibrates upon retrieve, the rattle sends out sound vibrations that help a fish locate it and, presumably, arouse the fish to strike. These innovations are actually on the fringe of the art of calling. I have no doubt that before long the sounds fish make, possibly not within the range of the human ear, will be deciphered by electronic equipment and played back perhaps with such devastating effect that their use by sport fishermen will have to be regulated.

What do the croakings and boomings of frogs mean? Do they find each other and converse in a simple language this way? Could a bullfrog be brought hopping to a hunter after its delectable legs? Maybe it could, if we understood how — and perhaps one day we may. But consider the fact that, as a greater need for management of all life forms becomes even more vital, calls of various kinds just may become valuable management tools. Calls are valuable to a small extent today, such as in the control of specific

Hawks come to predator calls as well as to calls that imitate hawks. Hawk calls, in turn, can be used to frighten pheasants and quail, as well as to arouse crows.

predators (see Chapter 12) that have become stock killers. Various animal populations may one day be surveyed and monitored by use of calls that are literally infallible in their mesmerism.

In devising new calling methods, we have to think in terms of appealing to every animal emotion, overlooking none. Hunger, the sex drive, competition, companionship, fright—all these of course are already the basis of various calls.

To illustrate the wide reach of these calls, I can note a call now available from Herter's for cottontail hunters that could also be used by photographers, or someone desiring to make a cottontail population survey. Cottontails are silent animals except for their death cries of anguish. They *frighten* rather easily, and the call causes fright. Termed the "Rabbit Flusher," this call emits a high-pitched, piercing cry. Herter's claims that where rabbits sit tight and a hunter is without a dog, a few blasts on this call will jump every rabbit within twenty yards or so. Thus, through fright, they are prompted to expose themselves, fleeing their brushy sanctuary.

169

Although this general principle has been pursued with some success with other creatures, who knows how far it might go if pondered and tried in other cases? Is there a sound that might drive rattlesnakes out of a thornbrush patch? Or one that might be used efficiently for rat control in a slum? Come to think of it, the Pied Piper, according to legend did quite a masterful job on both rats and children! The point is, in the future there may be more serious uses for calls than just for recreation.

CALLING IN AFRICA

Although various crude calling techniques have been practiced in Europe and elsewhere over the world, it is here in the United States that bird and animal calling have been brought to the highest stage of development. It is therefore somewhat paradoxical that American sportsmen, who travel more widely over the world after trophies than do citizens of any other country, have been slow to seize upon calling as a tool for greater success in other lands. Africa is possibly the classic example. The African safari has been a cynosure for thousands of American hunters and photographers. But they, and the white-hunters who guide them, have paid no attention at all to the use of calls.

However, poachers in Africa have used crude calling techniques for years, and the white hunters even know some of these tricks. I recall reading in *Outdoor Life* magazine about an experience Peter Barrett had while attempting to photograph a black rhino. His guide told him he could bring the great beast in close, if Pete desired it, by using a trick used by poachers. Pete was disbelieving, but got his cameras ready. The guide made several whining grunts and a repeated *whoosh* of breath. The enormous rhino stuck its tail up and came lumbering right at them. The guide repeated until it was a whole lot closer than the photographer wished it was!

The Burnham brothers of Marble Falls, Texas, mentioned frequently in this book, are nationally renowned for their calling abilities and their calls. They have pursued the idea of using calls in Africa and elsewhere farther than any other callers I know of. Several years ago they made a trip to Uganda purposely to see for themselves what their calls would do there. But they had been severely discouraged beforehand. They made a point of talking to a number of American hunters who had made safaris. When calls were mentioned, every one of them said there was no use. Calls simply would not work there. The Burnhams contacted several white hunters and were told the same thing.

So, they went on their own, and the upshot was that the reason calls didn't work in Africa was that nobody was using them. The Burnhams rented a vehicle and hired a cook and simply took off to test their calls. On the very first attempt, leaving the cook and all-round camp hand in the vehicle, they walked some distance away and began calling. They were using the identical call that they used back home in Texas to call coyotes, bobcats and foxes. The cook was startled to see two lions go bounding past, headed straight for the sound.

He saw them slow and begin a stalk. Alarmed, he started the vehicle and ran at them, yelling. The Burnhams were angry at the interruption, until they discovered that they had almost become lion bait. Later they were to call up and bag an enormous male lion. The popular fallacy of calls not producing in Africa was shattered.

During their stay they had two different leopards respond. But they were handicapped because they were not allowed to hunt at night. Their opinion is that leopards would be easy to call, from dusk on. But they felt it would be far too risky to try it without a gun, which they wangled permission to do.

It must be remembered that African animals—and other animals in foreign lands—have no knowledge of calls and thus many of them are totally naive. But it is interesting to note that the injured rabbit squall got results in Africa as efficiently as in the United States. It may be that animals

In spite of advice to the contrary, the author's friends, the Burnham brothers, traveled to Africa to experiment. Basic U.S. predator calls got strong responses, sometimes to the peril of the callers, and proved that animals everywhere can be called. Here jackals anticipate an easy meal.

there do not recognize it as a rabbit scream. But it certainly is recognizable as the cry of some forage creature in dire trouble. The Burnhams told me that they could not keep jackals away; the animals practically fell over each other trying to get to the call.

Curiously, the Burnhams discovered that various horned game also was intrigued. Lesser kudu, reedbuck, oribi, duiker, bushbuck, all came on the run. Topi and the tiny dik-dik responded eagerly. In fact, the boys took several trophies of horned game by calling. They found that elephants, giraffes, and even buffalo were curious.

When calling for predators, whether in America or elsewhere, one of the most dramatic facets of the endeavor is that the *caller* is the one being *hunted*. There is not too much actual danger to the caller in this country, but with the African lions and leopards there certainly is. The Burnhams called up a number of lions, but admitted they were a little skittish of just where and how to sit to keep from being the prey.

Even after their affirmative experience, the several outfitters they talked to seemed to take it all with a grain of salt and to have, as the Burnhams put it, mostly contempt for the whole idea. But the fact is, calling offers a whole new vista for hunters or photographers going to foreign lands — an oyster with a pearl in it just waiting to be opened.

IN CLOSING: AN INVITATION

In closing this book, I hope that all of this will give readers the desire to extend the frontiers of calling. Even with all that we already know, on a world scale, perhaps only the surface has been scratched. Bringing animals and birds or other creatures to you, or encouraging them to expose themselves to your view by appealing to one or another of their senses is an intensely provocative avocation. You do not need to be a hunter with gun or bow; although if you are, your success will be heightened by broad knowledge of calling. If you are a nonhunter, a hunter only with a camera, or just one hunting for the pure pleasure and thrills in observing wildlife, calling can be your hobby, too. Learning how to call animals and birds adds a vast new dimension to one's experiences with wildlife.

Photo Credits

Credit for photos of calling instruments goes to manufacturers noted in the photo captions. The author made all other photos with the exception of those listed below:

BURNHAM BROTHERS: pages 103, 146, 148 (top & middle), 151 (top), 162, 163, 164, 165, 169, 171

JAMES R. OLT: pages 7, 13, 43, 44, 58, 62, 140, 149

LEONARD LEE RUE III: pages 66 (top), 129, 135 (top)

JOHNNY STEWART: pages 121, 131, 153, 155 (A)

Index

Bobcats (*continued*)
  night calling for, 162, 163
  reactions when called, 20, 148,
    150, 151
  tracks, 158
  urine scents and, 33
Bobwhite quail, 77–80, 83
Brants, 59, 57
Breeze direction, 31–32
Buffalo, 9
Bullfrogs, 168
Burnham, Murry, 33, 81, 106, 109,
    130, 146, 147, 152, 154, 158,
    159, 162, 163, 170–171, 172
Burnham, Winston, 33, 81, 82, 103,
    106, 109, 147, 150, 152, 154,
    156, 158, 159, 162, 163, 170–
    171, 172
Burt, Ted, 113, 114, 119

California quail, 82–83
Calls:
  bellows type, 140, 141
  blue quail, 80–82
  bobcat, 146
  bobwhite quail, 78–80, 83
  California quail, 82–83
  cedar box, 69, 70, 71
  coyote, 146
  crow, 95, 96–97, 98
  deer, 104–106
  diaphragm, 69, 73
  dove, 89
  duck, 50–55
  elk, 115–116, 117
  fox, 146
  friction-type, 69
  Gambel's quail, 83, 84
  goose, 50, 52–53, 55–57
  javelina, 130, 131, 132
  moose, 122
  mountain quail, 84

mule deer, 103, 105–106
partridge, 87
pheasant, 85–87
predator, 130, 131, 132
rabbit, 145, 149–150, 154, 157,
    158, 169–170, 171–172
slate-and-striker, 69, 70, 71
squeaker, 154–156
squeeze bulb, 139
squirrel, 138–144
striker, 69, 70, 71, 138
turkey, 68–74
upland bird, 77, 83
yelper, 69, 73
Camouflage, *see* Concealment
Canvasbacks, 49, 54–55
Caribou, 7, 128–129
Carp, 5
Cedar box call, 69, 70, 71
Chachalacas, 161–162
Chukar partridge, 35, 87
Cinnamon teal, 49
Clothing, camouflage, 34–37, 157
Common Canada goose, 50, 52, 56,
    57
Concealment, 23–40
  blinds, 44–47, 94
  camouflage basics, 23–27
  clothing, 34–37, 157
  from ducks, 27, 41–47
  errors, 40
  from geese, 27, 41–47
  landscape features, utilizing, 24–
    27, 39
  of movement, 27–29
  rules, 38–39
  scent of caller, 31–34
  stands, 29–31
  from turkeys, 27, 74–75
  wariness cycle, 34
  from waterfowl, 26–27, 39, 41–
    47
Cottontails, *see* Rabbits